In the Grip of Grief

INDIGORIVER
PUBLISHING

IN THE GRIP OF GRIEF

A Family Memoir

TOM KNOX

In the Grip of Grief

Library of Congress Control Number: 2026901529
ISBN: 978-1-969935-28-2 (paperback) 978-1-969935-29-9 (ebook)

This book reflects the lived experience of grief shaped by the author's memory and the memories of those who contributed to the text. Some names and details were changed to protect privacy, and all contributions, including journal entries, were edited for clarity and brevity.

Editors: David Jorge Remy, Deborah Froese
Cover and Interior Design: Emma Elzinga

Printed in the United States of America

First Edition

3 West Garden Street, Ste. 718
Pensacola, FL 32502
www.indigoriverpublishing.com

Ordering Information:

Quantity sales: Special discounts are available on quantity purchases by corporations, associations, and others. For details, contact the publisher at the address above.

Orders by US trade bookstores and wholesalers: Please contact the publisher at the address above.

To my wife and best friend, Joyce, who endures with me as we journey together in our grief.

To our son Scott, who has lost so much yet perseveres. As Heather would say, "I'm so proud of you."

Grief and resilience live together.

– Michelle Obama

That which does not kill us makes us stronger.

– Friedrich Nietzsche

Contents

A Road That Never Ends

It has taken over twenty-five years for me to write about the death of my daughter, Heather. A lot has happened in our family since that catastrophic event rocked our world on May 27, 1999, but the grip of grief is still firm. Although this story is about the impact grief has on a family after the loss of a child, grief can impact anyone experiencing a severed relationship. The circumstances may be different, but grief holds tightly regardless. If you are experiencing a significant loss or life-changing event, I hope you will find nuggets of truth in this book to loosen that grip.

After Heather's death, I scouted for material that would help me come to terms with grief. I couldn't find much to comfort me, because at that time, my primary motivation was to avoid feeling so sad. I read clinical, medical, mystical, and religious perspectives. I read perspectives from well-meaning authors who had never experienced the emotions that accompany grief. I decided that if I ever wrote about our grief experience, it would not mirror anything I had read. Instead, it would reflect on personal experience and include information and feedback from our family dynamics.

The Grip of Grief is not a guidebook designed to take the reader through a process or a series of steps to help cope with or get over grief. Personally, I find this task to be very challenging. Many folks have written excellent material designed to help people cope. While I'm certain the approach taken by those authors was helpful for some, it wasn't beneficial for me.

Grief experiences are unique; there is no one-size-fits-all approach. That was true even in our close-knit family. Although we all experienced the same event, we reacted to it in different ways.

I decided to write this memoir as a family story because, for me, that makes the most sense. Family stories are based on shared experiences, filled with both positive and negative memories, viewed from different perspectives. Each family member contributes to each event. Some events occur while living under the same roof, and others take place when family members mature and separate from the central family unit. Telling our family story is like that.

In this book, stories about living with and adapting to grief after the death of my daughter, Heather, are told by people traveling this grief journey together. These main characters include Joyce, Heather's mom; Scott, her brother; Angela, Scott's wife; Donnie, Heather's widower; Jakob, her son; Debbie, her cousin; Mary Ann, her best friend; and me, Tom, her father.

Throughout my military and human resources career, I often conveyed teaching points by sharing stories of work-related events. And you could say that storytelling became part of my family's DNA. We made up stories when we traveled long distances, and we continued that practice with our grandchildren, Jakob and Leighton. Jakob, Heather and Donnie's child, was born on August 18, 1998, and experienced his mother's loss firsthand. Leighton, Scott and Angela's daughter, was born

February 5, 2010, and experienced Heather's loss through shared family stories.

Jakob's personal story has had a significant impact on our ability to cope with grief. In 2016, while Joyce and I visited him during a semester break at the University of Central Florida in Orlando, Jakob informed us that he was an atheist. I was so dumbfounded that I probably appeared catatonic. I felt as much confusion and disbelief as I'd experienced when I learned of Heather's accident, but with significant differences. Jakob grew up in a faith-filled home, yet he stepped away from our influence, role modeling, and training. We could have turned our backs on him and forfeited any opportunity to have a relationship, but we chose not to do that.

Two years later, Jakob announced that he was transgender and wanted to be referred to as *Jamie.* Not only were we grieving Heather's loss, but now we must adjust to having an atheist, transgender granddaughter. With all this chaos, we felt as though a weapon of mass destruction had been unleashed on our spirits. Nothing had prepared us for the emotional trauma we were experiencing. Perhaps a diagnosis of post-traumatic stress disorder (PTSD) would be appropriate. Since we had raised our grandchild as Jakob, we found it difficult to use another name, but we're honoring her desire to be called *Jamie*. Jakob and Jamie are the same person.

During the ensuing months, Joyce and I arrived at a point where, despite our limited understanding, we wholeheartedly accepted Jamie as a child of God. I take comfort in the fact that God does not turn his back on his creation and allows us to move through life as best we can, trusting in his grace. Jamie is gifted intellectually with an amazing capacity to serve others and lives by a well-defined moral compass. With a heart like hers, I cannot imagine that our God considers her unworthy. We love our granddaughter and will do all we can to assure her of our love. We don't fully understand LGBTQ issues, but we will continue to discuss, research, and study them. Jamie leads a productive life, is well-regarded by her peers, and is highly conscientious.

In the Grip of Grief is organized into chapters that explore the depth of our familial loss, concluding with lessons learned, Heather's legacy, and some resources you may find helpful if you are grieving too. There is even a favorite family recipe for muffins that Heather shared.

The first chapter belongs to Heather, as her life is at the core of our experiences. Subsequent chapters share select journal entries I wrote in the aftermath of Heather's death that reveal the conflicting emotions and turmoil of grief, and personal reflections from those who knew and loved Heather. Each of their narratives contributes a different story of loss and grief, a piece of a puzzle that comes together through trial and error. I hope that, through our stories, you will understand the lasting impact of grief. If our experience helps just one person feel less alone in their journey, the book will be a success.

A Beloved Life Remembered

Heather Denise Barber (nee Knox), daughter, sister, wife, mother.
June 29, 1971 - May 27, 1999

In June 1971, while I was training to become an Army Ranger at Ft Benning, Georgia, a very pregnant Joyce went to stay with her sister, Gladys, in Huntsville, Alabama. I couldn't wait to call and check on Joyce after completing my training. Gladys informed me that Joyce had been taken to the hospital to give birth. I immediately requested permission to leave to be with Joyce during her delivery. My commander informed me that, unless there were complications, I would have to stay and participate in a graduation ceremony.

As an obedient second lieutenant, I missed my daughter's birth, but once the graduation ceremony concluded, I raced to Huntsville Hospital to see Joyce and meet Heather.

During our pregnancy, Joyce and I were fond of discussing baby names. We had no clue as to the sex of the little person growing in her womb. We decided to name a baby girl, Heather Denise, but we couldn't agree on a boy's name. Upon arrival at the hospital, I briefly spoke with Joyce but could not wait to see my daughter. I secretly longed for a son, but when I saw Heather, any disappointment vanished. She was so tiny! Joyce was afraid that I wouldn't think Heather was a beautiful baby, but I saw a tiny, beautiful little girl, and I was in love.

Shortly after my arrival, the medical staff informed us that Heather wasn't gaining weight. A nurse discovered that Heather had a cleft upper palate and was unable to suck on a bottle to receive much-needed nourishment. (Fortunately, the cleft did not extend through her upper lip, which would have worsened the situation.) Additionally, Heather had jaundice and had to be placed under a special light to mitigate adverse effects on her liver.

What did all this mean? As new parents, we were mortified. Would Heather survive? How soon before we could take her home?

The jaundice was the least of our worries. The lack of weight gain was the real issue, and before we could take her home, the staff needed to figure out how to feed Heather. Fortunately, a nurse in the neonatal intensive care unit (NICU) discovered a way to bottle-feed her, and we took Heather home after a week in the hospital.

Her palate could be repaired through surgery, but the surgery would have to wait until she was a little older. When she was eighteen months old, she and Joyce went to Walter Reed Hospital in Washington, DC, for surgery to close her upper palate. During a post-operation consultation, Joyce was informed that Heather would probably need speech therapy.

When Heather started the first grade, Joyce asked Heather's teacher to let us know if she thought Heather would benefit from speech therapy because of her cleft palate. The teacher was shocked at the request. In her vast experience, Heather's speech was no different from that of other young children.

Heather never had a day of speech therapy.

When Heather was eight years old, she tripped over the end of a coffee table and ruptured her spleen. A clot developed that prevented internal bleeding. Had it not been for an emergency room doctor who thought it might be prudent to keep her in the hospital overnight; she may not have survived. Subsequent blood tests indicated that a splenectomy was imminent. During her recovery, the medical staff informed us that, without a spleen, there was a strong likelihood that she would be susceptible to infections. As she grew and matured, she led a healthy life and was no more susceptible to illness than her peers. It seems ironic that she survived two serious life-threatening medical-related issues only to die in an accident.

Heather wasn't precocious, but she had a strong work ethic that drove her to take on challenges and succeed. Her zest for life made her willing to try new things. She was a good athlete, excelled in swimming, and sometimes embarrassed the boys when they took her on in racquetball. She was a delight to be around and developed a strong faith. She also proved to be a good social etiquette coach and regularly trained her brother, Scott, who was three years younger. He routinely asked Heather questions about how to treat girls on a date.

In our home, there was never a shortage of laughter. Heather liked to pull pranks. One evening in high school, she and her best friend, Mary Ann, decided to cover a friend's yard with toilet paper. The outcome was a total disaster. The young man whose yard they rolled was not thrilled. Consequently, he and a buddy pursued Heather and Mary Ann as they drove away. When they caught up with the pair of vandals, one of the guys brandished a pistol. The girls were scared out of their minds! Reluctantly, she told me of the incident, worried I would do something drastic.

It wasn't usual for the trees in our yard to be rolled as neighborhood boys tried to get Heather and Mary Ann's attention. Conveniently, Heather always had something else on the go when it came time for the clean-up. Dad and brother pulled shreds of toilet paper from the big oak in our front yard.

It wasn't uncommon for Heather to pop out of a closet in an attempt to scare me. Or set up elaborate jokes, including "faking" a female admirer. On one April Fool's Day during her college years, she called to say she'd been in a car accident. She was fine, but the car was badly damaged. After asking a few questions, her roommate began to giggle in the background, and she had me. "April Fools!"

As much as Heather liked to have fun, she was no stranger to hard work. She excelled as a singer and musician, playing both flute and piano. She and Mary Ann visited nursing homes on weekends to perform for the residents. She wanted to attend the University of Alabama in Tuscaloosa, but she was disappointed when we guided her toward Harding University in Searcy, Arkansas. We knew we would miss her, but we thought Harding had much to offer.

At Harding, Heather was involved in various student activities. She became lifelong friends with her roommate Melanie, studied nursing, graduated as a registered nurse, and met her husband, Donnie Barber, an upperclassman from Fort Walton Beach, Florida.

Heather told entertaining stories about the extent and techniques boys used to get her attention. They were surprised that she was never shocked by their silly behavior and just ignored them. She was fond of telling them there was little they could do to get her attention. After all, she had a brother whose pranks gave her insight into how boys think and act.

Donnie was the exception.

Oddly enough, we sensed a connection between the two of them when we first met Donnie, but Heather insisted, "There just isn't any chemistry." She also said he seemed to know how to treat a woman. An upper-class man, he had a level of maturity her classmates lacked. He was smart, worked hard, and showed promise as a builder in his father's construction company even before he graduated from university.

Heather loved being a nurse and specialized in pediatrics. After she and Donnie married, she worked for Sacred Heart Hospital in Pensacola, Florida, where she launched a pediatric home care initiative. Donnie worked with his dad in residential and commercial construction along the Florida Panhandle.

The happy couple lived in Navarre, Florida. On August 18, 1998, shortly after moving into a home Donnie had remodeled, they were blessed with Jakob.

And now, with Jackob, Heather and Donnie become three.

They were so happy about the baby's arrival that they considered expanding their family. Joyce and I excitedly anticipated spending time with the young family. We lived three hundred miles away in Northport, Alabama, where Joyce worked as the registrar for Tuscaloosa County High School—Heather's and Scott's alma mater—and I was the personnel director for the City of Northport after retiring from the army. We began planning how we could move closer as their family grew.

Our lives were filled with joy. We regularly reflected on how blessed we were. We had raised two amazing kids. Heather was a nurse, and Scott was completing his studies to become a physical therapist. Then, we had our first grandchild. Life was perfect . . . until it wasn't.

Nothing Joyce or I had experienced prepared us for the phone call we received from Donnie on Thursday, May 27, 1999. Heather and Jakob had been in an accident while returning home from the post office in Gulf Breeze, Florida. Haltingly, Donnie told us that Heather had died. Jakob was okay. Shock and awe infused our bodies, and for a while, we were paralyzed. No expression adequately describes our bewilderment and pain, or the overwhelming numbness.

Once we began to comprehend that our daughter was dead, we left Tuscaloosa to be with Donnie and Jakob, but we clung to denial until we arrived at the hospital. Then, the reality of the situation confronted us.

Even though we were grateful that Jakob survived, grief exerted an unrelenting grip on our hearts and minds.

Thus begins our family's story.

Journaling Through Grief

Trying to make sense of my grief, I discovered information on journaling that promoted the idea of using pen and paper to adjust to a significant life change, cope with anxiety, and manage stress. Because of the grip grief had on me, I decided to give journaling a shot. So, in October 1999, I began journaling and kept it up until 2003 when it had served its purpose.

At first, I wrote diligently, but over time, I began writing less and less unless there was something significant to write about. Many of my entries bear witness to my deep emotional wounds. Those entries express sorrow, anger, love, regret, anticipation, and confusion. At the time, I didn't realize that much of my writing was a journey of self-discovery. I sincerely hope that someone will be able to relate, find comfort, and perhaps inspiration from my experiences.

I started writing *In the Grip of Grief* to provide a resource with broad appeal to others who suffered like me. I didn't intend to write from a religious or biblical perspective, not only because I was so angry with God, but because I wanted the book to appeal to atheists, agnostics, and people from a wide array of faiths. I thought quoting Scripture and using the Bible as the standard for managing grief might turn off people from other faith backgrounds. However, I soon discovered that my writing lacked authenticity because I downplayed the importance of my faith. As a result, my journal follows a path of spiritual navigation through grief. The rest of this chapter draws excerpts and insights from those writings that seem most relevant to my journey and reflect my tumultuous state of mind.

October 1999

Since Heather's death five months ago, on May 27, I have been lost and consumed with indescribable pain. I came across a Book by Zig Ziglar entitled *Confessions of a Grieving Christian.*[1] The book expresses his thoughts on losing his daughter to chronic obstructive pulmonary disease (COPD). I found some measure of comfort in his observation that his grief was directly proportional to the love he felt for his daughter—until it dawned on me that grieving so deeply was almost like punishment for loving deeply.

Some days, I close the door to my office, hoping no one will come by, and sit in silence and sob. I almost hate to be alone, for then sadness envelopes me, especially when I go to the cemetery to visit her grave. Just seeing her grave results in waves of sorrow. It's like being at the beach. Waves come in and then retreat. Cleansing takes place when they recede.

Sometimes, when grief isn't incapacitating me, I almost feel guilty. I have the nagging feeling that maybe I don't miss her. It's almost as though I *need* to miss her to enjoy her memory.

---

1 Zig Ziglar, *Confessions of a Grieving Christian* (Thomas Nelson Inc; Revised edition, 1999).

November 1999

Often, despite my fury toward God, I attempt to draw closer to him for comfort—quite the paradox. Support comes in other ways too. Joyce's sister Bobbie has been a rock. She listens and offers encouragement. My son doesn't seem able to offer much encouragement. Scott's own grief doesn't leave room for anything but wrestling with Heather's loss. He won't visit the cemetery with Joyce or me but chooses to go alone instead.

I often refer to Heather in the first person. When asked how many children I have, I responded by saying *two*. There is no need to say one of them is dead. All I want to do is hold Heather, talk with her, and tease her.

Will that desire ever vanish?

It's my nature to do whatever I can to survive. It brings emotional turmoil. Whenever my pain is so great that I think God could easily end it by just whisking me away, I feel selfish. Another wave of guilt follows. Joyce, Scott, and Jakob need me.

A battle between two forces rages within me: logic and feeling. Sometimes, when emotions associated with grief appear, I want to wrestle them away, head-on. At other times, I actively look for grief because in that grief, pleasant emotions associated with my memory of Heather reside. In some bizarre sense, my pain honors her memory. From a logical perspective, none of this makes sense. The pain hasn't lessened, and she is still gone, yet a feeling of peace often follows wrestling. Maybe it's like fighting a battle or competing in an event. Calmness enters the soul when it's over. Perhaps I'm like an addict who does whatever it takes to get high on grief, my drug of choice.

After writing those words, they seem a little weird.

Maybe experiencing grief brings spiritual growth. Perhaps, in time, I'll be able to tell if any growth has occurred. In the meantime, I chose LFTEG—the acronym for "learn from today's experience and grow"—to use as my computer login.

Jakob is now fifteen months old, and I'm compelled to ensure our grandchild has a bright future. In my arrogance, I keep thinking I'm the instrument to make that happen, but at the same time, I cannot do it alone. God will lead me in the right direction.

Even though Jakob stays with Joyce and me, we feel it's important for him to spend as much time with his father as possible. Since Donnie works in Fort Walton with his dad, Joyce and Jakob often spend weeks at a time there. I don't like my separation from Joyce; I draw strength from being with her.

A friend read somewhere that when a child dies, the marriage often crumbles. Whether true or not, this observation is an incentive for me. I won't want Heather's death to result in problems with our marriage. There is no way I could make this journey alone. Joyce is also under a lot of stress too, and I want to be supportive. We draw strength from one another.

It's also essential for us to eat well, sleep well, and exercise.

Go figure, I almost sound like a coach!

The holidays are just around the corner, and we dread our first holiday without Heather. Anticipation is the worst part. I still find it hard to accept that my daughter is in a hole in the ground.

With Joyce in Fort Walton looking after Jakob, I'm not fit for any company. I'm angry with God because nothing is working out. I can't hold Joyce to console her, even though I'm worried about her. That creates a lot of anxiety. I'm concerned about Joyce taking on the role of mother to Jakob in Heather's stead. I worry about Jakob's welfare, our possible relocation, finding a job, finding a congregation to worship with, Scott's education in physical therapy school, and our health.

At times, I feel helpless and want to give up, although I don't tend toward depression. But depression runs in Joyce's family, and that worries me. It's frustrating to have no idea about what our new future holds while knowing the plans we made are ruined.

I feel like a hypocrite. I may appear normal, but when I'm alone, I feel more like a zombie. People may think my faith is intact, but I constantly question God in my anger. Who else can I blame for Heather's death? Certainly not the young man who ran her off the road. It was just an accident.

With all these emotions storming inside me, I'm ashamed to pray, because I'm not sure I believe what I'm saying. I'm not even sure what I'm feeling. My mood is impacted by what Joyce is experiencing. I think we're being tested. No matter what we've been taught, with Heather's loss, we have been given much more than we can endure. We're told not to worry about anything over which we have little control. To that end, we may be creating a lot of stress for ourselves by trying to control our emotions and seeking answers to the big WHY.

Joyce is driven to do whatever is necessary to be with Jakob, even if it means separation from me. What if her drive and energy don't lead to the outcome she anticipates? Will she feel she has disappointed Heather, or will she feel her efforts were useless? The stress created by her worry will cause her to age, and she might develop health issues, and I'll have to put her in an early grave too.

Isn't the same happening to me?

We need to wake up to these possibilities and prevent them from happening. Our focus needs to be taking care of ourselves.

Our misery may not result in our marriage dissolving but it could dissolve into a platonic relationship. Unlike me, Joyce is the epitome of a multitasker, but she has reached her limit. I know she thinks about us, but our relationship is not a priority for her right now.

My optimistic nature is being challenged. I'm becoming pessimistic about our relationship, our ability to raise Jakob, the future, relocation, emotional support for Scott, and much more. I have no control over my life, and it's driving me crazy. If we were denied the opportunity of taking care of Jakob, the hit to Joyce would be catastrophic, and I would lose her emotionally, and she would withdraw into a shell. After a storm and the rain has cleansed the earth, the environment seems to be so fresh and peaceful. Does crying have the same effect on us? Goodness knows I have shed enough tears to last a lifetime.

Scott is a real casualty in this mess. He already lost his sister, and he could also lose his mom and dad. We stand to lose so much.

I often feel like I'm falling down a waterfall, tossing, tumbling, twisting at the whim of the water, totally out of control. It feels as though not even God is in control. We felt blessed by the awesome life we had before the accident, but now it seems like we're being punished for feeling so blessed. I'm not rejecting God. I just don't trust him like I used to. Maybe I'm a fair-weather Christian. Like a football fan, when things are going well and the team is winning, we're excited and cheer; but when things don't go as we think they should, we lose interest in watching the game.

During the Thanksgiving holiday, I had to apologize to Joyce for acting like a turkey (ha-ha). I was consumed by remorse for being selfish and unkind to the most significant person in my life. Heather's death hit me so hard because she is such a big part of me. It does bring comfort to think that we're linked through our feelings, and that means Heather is always with me.

As a family, we were very happy before she died. Heather loved her job as a pediatric nurse and being a mom to Jakob. Scott was in physical therapy school after a successful career playing football for Samford University in Birmingham, and we enjoyed our regular visits to Pensacola. A parent never stops loving a child; it must be like that with God. He never stops loving us.

December 1999

Joyce and I had been married a little over a month when we found out we were pregnant. We were upset and cried. In the blink of an eye, our lives changed. We knew we would have kids eventually, but we wanted to adjust to one another before we entered parenthood. But there was no turning back. Our adventure began as a young couple with a baby on the way and the start of my military service.

When we told friends about the pregnancy, their reactions delighted me. I could tell they were doing the mental math, wondering if Joyce had conceived before the wedding, which wasn't the case.

Heather was part of our entire married life. On our first Christmas together, she was in Joyce's womb. And now, this coming Christmas will be our first without her. How ironic is that? What are the odds that one person can cause two life-altering changes at the same time of year in two other people? The little girl who changed our lives forever has gone and done it again. The latest change is far more significant than the first one because this one will be harder to adjust to.

Last night, I visited Mary Gibson, a dear friend in the hospital. She introduced me to Bishop Ernest Palmer, who was also there, and Mary mentioned my loss. When I made a few comments about how I felt, he responded with two statements I'll never forget. They've given me tremendous comfort.

1. It's obvious that Heather loved life: she loved and is loved, she is remembered, and she was a servant.
2. I was making it through my grief because I didn't dwell on the accident when I told him about it. I spent most of my time talking about Jakob and Heather.

On my road trips to be with Joyce and Jakob in Fort Walton, I would reflect on how honored we should feel by the tributes that pour in for Heather. She left an amazing legacy. Maybe God allows things like this, so we won't get stuck in our grief, knowing that Heather made a difference in the lives of other people. It struck me that God disrupts our plans to stretch us. From her conception to her death, Heather changed our lives.

For a person who requires lots of sleep, Joyce has plenty of energy in her role as a mother to Jakob. She also has back issues, but she doesn't seem to have any problem when she must carry Jakob.

Many of our family and friends think the responsibility for Jakob rests with Donnie, Heather's widower, but with Donnie's permission, we know we're doing what needs to be done for Jakob's welfare. While some people question our decision to be caregivers for Jakob, others have recognized our role.

Scott gave me a real boost the other night when he said that he loved me and that I was the best dad in the world. He mentioned Cat Stephens's song, "Father and Son," about spending time together. In one verse, the son says, "This has been the best day of my life."[2] It reminded me of a time when I took Heather fishing as a junior high student. She told me that it didn't matter how many fish we caught. "What is important is that I'm with you, and we're together outdoors."

Another great song is "Fathers and Daughters" by Michael Bolton. Although listening to these songs and others causes grief to wash over me, I still find them worth listening to.

Just before Heather's accident, Joyce and I planned to visit Pensacola. We got up Saturday morning, a week before our intended departure, and said, "What the heck, let's go see the kids now." And so, we did. It turned out to be a blessing that we went. It was the last time we saw Heather alive. The following Thursday, we were notified of her accident.

Before the accident, Sacred Heart had taken some pictures of Heather to use in some of their promotional material for pediatrics. One of their most used photos captured her wearing scrubs and holding Jakob during a break when she left the hospital to visit him in daycare.

Just before the accident.

2 Cat Stevens, *Father and Son*, lyrics, in *Tea for the Tillerman* (Island Records, 1970).

Adding the component of grief to our lives requires an unusual set of coping skills. But because grief is rarely anticipated, there isn't any training available to prepare for it. We must improvise and adapt to grief, but we will never overcome it.

Our family has successfully dealt with all manner of challenges: Heather being born with a cleft palate, lots of family relocations (some military moves, at least one to find a new job), many separations, marriages, serious surgeries (Heather's cleft palate repair and her splenectomy when she was eight years old—we almost lost her), empty nesting, grandchildren, and now grief.

Really?

The energy it takes to deal with grief is draining. As much as I would have liked God to prevent the tragedy of her death, He cannot suspend the natural laws for just one person—or for one family. It gives me some measure of comfort knowing that God is aware of the pain her loss caused, while also knowing her purpose in this life was complete. It was time for her to go to her forever home.

This time of year, with its emphasis on family, reminds me that ours is fractured. Seasons will come and go, events will be anticipated long before their arrival and then become history, but memories will not fade.

At least for us, they will not.

January 2000

Donnie appears reluctant to move to Tuscaloosa to be close to Joyce and me; consequently, I'll have to find a job in Pensacola to honor our commitment to help him raise Jakob. I'm being forced to leave a great job where I work with amazing people and a community where we anticipated retiring. A picture of Jakob in one of my shirt pockets reminded me of our commitment. We will just have to do what we think is right and trust that God will bless our efforts.

Our son mentioned that grief appears to act as an anchor, holding us back at times and preventing us from moving forward. We might also think of it as an anchor holding us steady as we attempt to navigate the future.

It's not unusual for people to offer kind words of encouragement. I almost feel these folks are ministering angels sent to lift me up. While at work, a friend called to tell me he was thinking of me and reminded me of a story from the Old Testament about Moses, Aaron, and Hur. When Moses held his arms up, the Israelites prevailed in their battle against the Amalekites. When his arms dropped, they began to lose. His friends were there to hold up his arms.

I get the point.

> [8]*The Amalekites came and attacked the Israelites at*
> *Rephidim.*[9] *Moses said to Joshua, "Choose some of our men*
> *and go out to fight the Amalekites. Tomorrow I'll stand on*
> *top of the hill with the staff of God in my hands."*
>
> [10]*So Joshua fought the Amalekites as Moses had ordered, and*
> *Moses, Aaron and Hur went to the top of the hill.* [11]*As long*
> *as Moses held up his hands, the Israelites were winning, but*
> *whenever he lowered his hands, the Amalekites were win-*
> *ning.* [12]*When Moses' hands grew tired, they took a stone and*
> *put it under him and he sat on it. Aaron and Hur held his*
> *hands up—one on one side, one on the other—so that his*
> *hands remained steady till sunset.* [13]*So Joshua overcame the*
> *Amalekite army with the sword* (Exodus 17: 8-13).

Joyce was a Tuscaloosa County High School administrator, well-regarded among other administrators, teachers, and staff. When they learned of Heather's death and that Joyce was caring for Jakob, they donated their personal time to cover her work so she wouldn't have to worry about a loss of income. After a year, she chose to step away from her job altogether and focus on Jacob.

When we decided to move, I had to give up my job too. When asked if it were best to leave a job I love to relocate and become a legal guardian for Jakob, in my arrogance, I said *yes*. No couple could raise Jakob better than us. But I'm being forced out of my comfort zone. Even in my anger, I remind myself that we need to be content and trust God because we don't have as much control as we think we do.

Joyce mentioned that she had difficulty resting, and in her disquiet, she heard Heather whisper that she needed to rest so she could better take care of Jakob. We discussed how even though we can't see Heather, we can feel her. Maybe that is because we have pictures and memories. She is just a thought away.

I had a tough week, probably because Jakob had gone with his dad to visit his aunt (his dad's sister) in New Jersey. I went to the cemetery, stood at the foot of Heather's marker, and wept. When I got home, Joyce sensed I was having a tough time and held me as I cried.

We're committed to helping Jakob get to know his mom as well as we do. Joyce and Heather are so much alike that this task should not be too difficult. Heather had Joyce's sensitivity toward others and her organizational skills. She was more like me with her sense of adventure and how she accepted challenges.

I'm coming around to the idea that God really cares for us. Joyce and I are both developing a sense of calm about the future.

Figure 3: Tom at the cemetery

Taking a break to visit Heather's grave.

It's almost as though God is telling us to put our energy into caring for Jakob, and he will work out the other details.

On our way to Pensacola this past weekend, we stopped by Pensacola Naval Air Station. Joyce and I had planned to live close to a military base when I retired to take advantage of the services offered. We also wanted to worship in a congregation that supported military families, so we could help others like we had been supported during my service and various assignments. We discovered the Gateway Church of Christ, where Donnie, Heather, and Jakob worshipped. So, despite the unexpected twist of grief in our lives, we found the military base and the church we had hoped for.

February 2000

I woke up feeling as though Heather was with me. When I remembered that was impossible, it felt like someone had thrown cold water in my face. After nearly nine months of grieving, I'm not in a better place.

Doubt is always present. Even though we have signs that God is watching over us, I continue to wonder if we're doing the right thing. Are we on an imaginary course we dreamed up? Maybe we're supposed to get on with our lives. I ask God for direction. Hopefully, God will rekindle our sense of purpose.

When I visit the cemetery nowadays, I notice that the dirt patch surrounding Heather's grave is turning to grass and blending in with the surrounding turf. In like manner, our lives are blending in with the other lives surrounding us. I guess this could mean that we're surviving despite the grip grief has on us.

The specter of grief lurks around each corner, just waiting to ambush me. The best thing to do in an ambush is to counterattack. When grief assails me, I manage to survive and continue to function. Through tearful acceptance of our grief, we somehow muddle through.

I was asked what it would be like to leave Northport and visit Heather's grave less frequently. I callously responded that Heather's grave is just a hole in the ground like any other. I'm not sure if I believe that. Even though it's just a hole in the ground where her physical remains rest, I visualize holding her small frame and pressing her head against my chest. If I could do that, I would say, "I love you and I'm so proud of you."

Heather was the tiniest family member. Joyce, Scott, and I were tall compared to her. When we were in the kitchen together, three of us would gather and start hugging and yelling, "Short circle." We would pull Heather into the middle, squeeze, and laugh.

Maybe the distraction of planning for our future is a good thing since it diverts attention from our grief journey. Grief does not lose its grip or its strength. The passage of time is not the key. Grief robs me of my ability to serve others effectively. I'm self-absorbed. I continue to feel conflicted. Is God rewarding us with the care of Jakob because we did a good job raising Heather and Scott? Or is he punishing us because we blew it, and giving us another chance at child rearing by pulling Jakob into our lives?

This is all beyond my comprehension.

Joyce said she would like to talk to Heather just one more time. I can only imagine how long that conversation would last. I try to console myself that Heather is just a thought away. If we could move beyond the physical and spend more time contemplating the spiritual, we would be better off. We all have the common bond of the Spirit. The same Spirit that ministered to us when our family was whole now ministers to us in our grief. There is comfort in knowing that even though we're separated, we're joined by a more powerful force than life.

It's interesting to note that we seem more receptive to the Spirit's voice when we're worshipping or at the cemetery.

March 2000

There are many times when the anger I direct toward God is proportional to the intensity of my love. Perhaps our strong calling to raise Jakob stems from what Heather told Donnie before the accident: if anything happened to her, she wanted us to help him raise Jakob.

Some people may realize that, despite my anger, I think God is worthy of praise, and despite all else, he has a strong track record. He has blessed us beyond measure, and I'm optimistic (because that is my nature) that I'll understand how truly good he is in time. How is it possible to be angry, feel abandoned, hurt, and filled with pain, and yet believe that God is good?

Joyce and I went to a meeting of Compassionate Friends. There were approximately twenty people there. Some had lost children as recently as we had, and some many years ago. The children varied in age at their deaths. The group was diverse, but we had one thing in common: our grief. Everyone seemed to accept that whatever it took to help us come to grips with grief was okay. We will probably attend another meeting in the future. It's perhaps the closest I'll come to group therapy.

One day, while leaving the cemetery, I heard Heather

whisper some Scripture that I had shared with her when she was young: Matthew 6: 25-34. Another “hello” from Heather. (From now on, whenever Joyce and I sense that Heather is close by, we will refer to it as a “Heather Hi.”)

> 25 *“Therefore I tell you, do not worry about your life, what you will eat or drink; or about your body, what you will wear. Is not life more than food, and the body more than clothes?* 26 *Look at the birds of the air; they do not sow or reap or store away in barns, and yet your heavenly Father feeds them. Are you not much more valuable than they?* 27 *Can any one of you by worrying add a single hour to your life[a]?*
>
> 28 *”And why do you worry about clothes? See how the flowers of the field grow. They do not labor or spin.* 29 *Yet I tell you that not even Solomon in all his splendor was dressed like one of these.* 30 *If that is how God clothes the grass of the field, which is here today and tomorrow is thrown into the fire, will he not much more clothe you—you of little faith?* 31 *So do not worry, saying, ‘What shall we eat?’ or ‘What shall we drink?’ or ‘What shall we wear?’* 32 *For the pagans run after all these things, and your heavenly Father knows that you need them.* 33 *But seek first his kingdom and his righteousness, and all these things will be given to you as well.* 34 *Therefore do not worry about tomorrow, for tomorrow will worry about itself. Each day has enough trouble of its own* (Matthew 6:25-34).

A few days ago, I went to the cemetery, and for some unknown reason, I felt more connected with Heather than usual.

And in that moment, a sense of peace fell over me when logically, I should have been falling apart. Considering our lives are bound by a rope of three strands—Heather, God, and me—we're weakened because one of the strands is missing. Yet God is not going to let that happen because his strand is ultimately holding everything together.

> [9] *Two are better than one,*
> *because they have a good return for their labor:*
> [10] *If either of them falls down,*
> *one can help the other up.*
> *But pity anyone who falls*
> *and has no one to help them up.*
> [11] *Also, if two lie down together, they will keep warm.*
> *But how can one keep warm alone?*
> [12] *Though one may be overpowered,*
> *two can defend themselves.*
> *A cord of three strands is not quickly broken*
> (Ecclesiastes 4:9-12).

My ache must be part of the healing process. An expression used during intense training and physical workouts may also be true in this case: "What doesn't kill you makes you stronger." Maybe the Spirit's whispering to me and saying, "You can't see her now, but in time you will." Those words give me hope beyond the grave.

Am I weeping for her loss or at the amazement of it all?

Our faith may waver despite everything, but it's not totally disappearing. Perhaps healing is not the right goal for us. Equipping might be better. We're becoming equipped to function despite the grip of grief's hold on us. Living with grief and dealing with all the situations we must deal with gives us a sense of purpose.

May 2000

I constantly pray that we will receive the knowledge and wisdom needed to control the situation. Often, we become frustrated. I pray that God will not let us be so uptight about our loss of Heather and the new responsibilities we have for raising Jakob.

It struck me that we're a bridge between Heather and Jakob. I think Heather appreciated her upbringing, and perhaps Donnie also sees qualities in us that he wants us to impart to Jakob. There is very little guessing on this front because we turn to God with the expectation that he will fix things. So much happens beyond our power to change or correct.

God has instilled in us the ability to know what to do. When we're scared, we hide. When we're weak, we seek strength. When we're sick physically or emotionally, we seek help to become well. It's no surprise to discover we lack power and have less control than we think we do.

What lessons are taught through our experiences, if any? How are we supposed to apply what we learn?

A good friend, Jim Wright, told me that by yearning to get closer to God, we were getting closer to Heather because we knew where God was, and she was with God. We can be closer to her in no other way. Jim is among many ministering angels.

We have survived one year only by God's grace. There is no other explanation. I'm curious whether the intensity of grief ever diminishes. Does pain serve a greater purpose? The thought struck me that we consist of 50 percent physical body and 50 percent Spirit. I'm not sure if that's accurate, but the notion that our equilibrium is disrupted when one part of us is out of balance seems to hold some truth. For me, the Spirit is undeniably part of us, a voice that I often don't hear or ignore. By failing to perceive the Spirit, I'm depriving myself of a lot I could benefit from. I firmly believe that Heather is experiencing a spirit-filled existence. Her body's limitations no longer shackle her. All I can do is yearn for the same freedom she has.

Someday, I hope to have the same joy she must be feeling.

September 2000

Because of our commitment to help raise Jakob, Joyce spends two weeks in Tuscaloosa and two weeks in Fort Walton. When she is in Tuscaloosa, she may be with me physically, but she is still thinking like a full-time mom. When she is in Fort Walton, three hundred miles lie between us. As much as I like to think we're okay, I can't help feeling that I'm not much help and I don't matter. My relationship with Joyce is suffering. Our separations over the past year have taken an emotional toll.

You would think that after thirty years of marriage, we would be equipped to weather any crisis that comes our way. Grief sucks! We love each other deeply and are determined to get things back on track. We're talking and sharing more and developing plans for our future—whatever it may hold—and we want God to be at the center of those plans.

It seems strange that not too long ago, I didn't want to have anything to do with God because of my anger. Since we have agreed that it's important for Jakob to know his dad, we're moving to the Florida Panhandle. As we plan our move, Donnie and I have decided that it might be a good idea to build two houses on adjacent lots, one for him and one for us. That would allow both of us to work while Joyce takes care of Jakob. I'm reluctant to do much planning until Donnie starts building.

The anticipated move has put us on a roller coaster ride of emotions. Some days we're in a deep valley of despair, wondering what we're supposed to do, and then every so often we get a whisper that inspires us.

OCTOBER 2000

At church one Sunday, we heard a reading from Deuteronomy 6:4-9, another one of Heather's favorite Old Testament scriptures. In fact, we found her Bible open to that Scripture on the day she died.

> [4]*Hear, O Israel: The Lord our God, the Lord is one. Love the Lord your God with all your heart and with all your soul and with all your strength. These commandments that I give you today are to be on your hearts. Impress them on your children. Talk about them when you sit at home and when you walk along the road, when you lie down and when you get up. Tie them as symbols on your hands and bind them on your foreheads. Write them on the doorframes of your houses and on your gates.* (Deuteronomy 6:4–9)

As I followed the reading in my Bible, I flipped over the bookmark made from one of her purple scrubs—her favorite color, and a part of her identity as a nurse. I'd had several bookmarks made from those scrubs to share with the family. On the back of mine is an inscription: *Tell Dad I love him.* Every phone call between Joyce and Heather ended with those words. And there it was, staring at me. Was this another Heather Hi?

Maybe I'm creating a type of fantasy when I attribute things that happen to a Heather Hi, but I don't think things happen by coincidence. I choose to attribute the gifts I occasionally reçeive to God. He's looking after me.

As it turns out, we found what we were looking for in a building lot. The kicker? It's located in the same subdivision where Donnie had planned to build a house for Heather, Jakob, and him as they grew their family. There must be something special about this place since Heather saw herself raising Jakob here. Now all I need is a job in Florida. I'm too young to retire, and we need the income. The cost of living is higher in Florida than in Alabama.

One morning, I awoke with the feeling that someone was watching over us, protecting and caring for us. We're still in a vulnerable emotional state, with our concerns for Donnie, Jakob, Scott, and the future, but even before getting out of bed, I was overcome with the feeling that all is well.

At dusk, just as some stars were becoming visible, Jakob stopped playing for a moment. He looked into the sky, pointed, and declared, "Heather Barber star."

Joyce and I were blown away. Later that evening, after Jakob was in bed, we looked at the Celestial Registry we had purchased several months ago to claim a star for Heather, and as we looked at it, we heard someone singing "Twinkle, Twinkle Little Star" on the Hallmark show we had been watching.

It was almost like getting a phone call from Heather, just to say hello.

I think we can expect Heather Hi's frequently.

November 2000

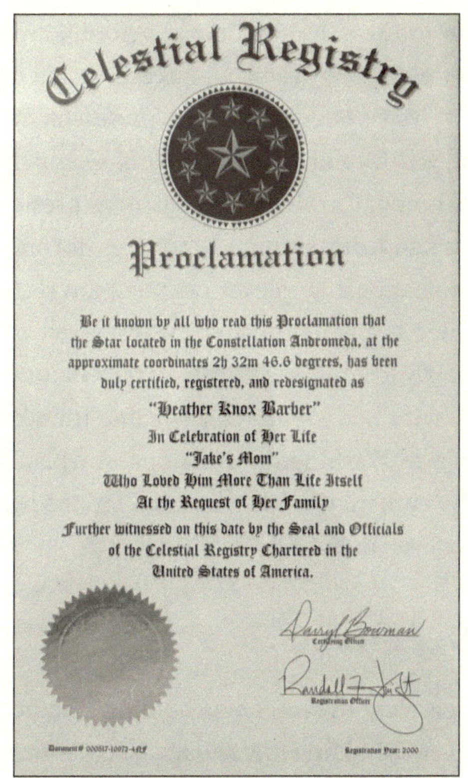

Celestial Registry

Proclamation

Be it known by all who read this Proclamation that the Star located in the Constellation Andromeda, at the approximate coordinates 2h 32m 46.6 degrees, has been duly certified, registered, and redesignated as

"Heather Knox Barber"

In Celebration of Her Life

"Jake's Mom"

Who Loved Him More Than Life Itself

At the Request of Her Family

Further witnessed on this date by the Seal and Officials of the Celestial Registry Chartered in the United States of America.

Certifying Officer

Registration Officer

Registration Year: 2000

Claiming a star to honor Heather.

I stopped by the cemetery before heading to the airport to catch my flight to Washington, DC, for the annual SHRM (Society for Human Resource Management) conference. Some purple daisy-like flowers were blooming in a pot tossed against a fence behind Heather's marker. The strangest part about all this was the weather. It was cool with drought-like conditions, and it wasn't the time of year for flowers to bloom. For some unknown reason, this small pot of purple flowers grew anyway.

After several moments of silence, I returned to the fence and gazed at those flowers to make certain I wasn't imagining them. I'm inclined to believe they were yet another Heather Hi.

On the plane, I met Mary and Carol. They were going to the same conference I planned to attend. Since I knew we would eventually move to Pensacola, I hoped to network during the conference and develop contacts who might be beneficial during my job search. I had never before networked to secure a job, so once again, I was being forced outside my comfort zone.

Mary is currently the president of the Pensacola Chapter of SHRM and covers Workers' Compensation for West Florida Hospital. Carol was the chapter's president-elect and employed by Landrum Human Resources, formally known as Amstaff, a professional employer organization (PEO). Carol had lost twins at birth, and her husband was severely injured in a car wreck. He nearly lost his life. It seemed only natural for me to share my story with her. We quickly became friends. God really blessed my trip to Washington. All along, my plan had been to network at the conference, but true connections began on the plane before we even arrived.

December 2000

In a vivid dream, I was holding Heather in my arms, or rather, she was holding me, and my face was buried in her neck. I felt her hair and smelled her perfume (Beautiful). I was so glad to see her and just wanted to keep holding her. Joyce called that a Heather Hi. I usually don't remember my dreams, but this one was so vivid it was hard to forget. I was determined to remember it.

I can barely function this time of year, knowing that Christmas was Heather's season. Christmas is now rough for us, and we have trouble thinking that God really understands our suffering; if he did, he would make it go away.

Christian grief literature tries to make us feel we're spiritually elite because we have suffered more than other Christians, and yet we still hold onto our faith. To me, that thought seems repugnant. I would rather not be chosen or considered a spiritual elite.

Our pain is incapacitating at times, but somehow, we survive. Maybe someday I'll have a better understanding of how our experience has helped us.

One thing I'm certain of: God expects me to question and search for answers and to be open-minded. Are things as they should be? Maybe in God's mind, but not in mine. I'm certain that some people accept things a lot easier than I do. I just want assurances that things at work now in our lives will bring us all to our eternal home, together. Scripture addresses this, but it's hard to accept what Scripture says.

Is that blasphemy? Maybe so, but it doesn't change my current view of things.

In another dream about Heather, she stood in our kitchen, dressed in Khaki shorts with a peach-colored top (I didn't think it was possible to dream in color). I remember looking at her, wanting to hold her and never let her go. At the same time, I knew it was a dream, and the vision would soon be gone. Of course, I wanted the dream to be a reality. I didn't want to go back to sleep. Joyce was in the dream also, but she was unaware of Heather's presence. It's like we were sharing the dream, but I knew something she didn't.

As strange as it may sound, I sensed I was crossing from one dimension into another with total awareness of what was going on in both dimensions. While I was with Heather, I knew she was dead . . . but *was* she dead? I was willing to give up my reality to be with her. Although both dimensions seemed real, the one where Heather was alive seemed the much better one to me. Although I could not smell her, I felt her hair once again. Perhaps my mind was playing tricks on me. I wonder if it's possible to be with her spirit and then come back to the reality I live in, knowing what I saw and how I felt.

The idea of perseverance through grief's pain may be part of what faith is all about. The word *steadfast* also comes to mind. Having the toughness and strength to endure through the hell we're going through *and* remain faithful is a mystery.

I wonder if we're in an elite group of special forces, fighting against the enemy of grief, because we're specially trained to do so. To be part of this special group, one must go through the experience (pain). It's kind of like boot camp. Everyone who served in the military has gone through boot camp; it's the common denominator that brings all service members together.

Maybe the expression "keep your friends close but keep your enemies closer" has an application when we consider a life filled with grief. My enemy is grief, and I know that he can launch an attack on my feelings at any time. There is nowhere to run. No place I can hide. Armed with this knowledge, I know it's okay to be sad, cry, and be angry. There is no fighting back. My biggest weapon is the fact that the grief attack will pass, and I'll press on, feeling that Heather is with me through all the turmoil.

Together, we won't let grief get a permanent grip on us.

January 2001

My birthday came and went, and for me it was a time of sorrow. The only thing that could have made my birthday joyful would have been hearing my princess say, "Happy Birthday, Daddy."

Impossible, but nonetheless, all I wanted.

Birthdays are not as exciting as they once were. It's like anticipating a favorite dish and finding out it has lost its flavor. Nothing in my life is as enjoyable and as rich as it once was, except worship, which has taken on a special significance.

Last weekend, we were in Pensacola and had supper with the Zeilers, a couple from Gateway Church. We told them I was thinking of beginning a job search, because it appeared moving was imminent. Richard offered to give my resume to a Pensacola business leader, Britt Landrum, when they got together for lunch the following week.

Britt owns Landrum Human Resources, the same company where Carol Cox works, the woman I met on my November trip to DC.

I told Joyce I felt compelled to put together a résumé even though I wasn't yet prepared to start job hunting. I broke all records preparing and mailing a hard copy of my résumé to Richard. The seed was planted. Would it germinate?

My question was answered quickly. Richard called to tell me to contact Mike Perkins, the VP for Operations at Landrum Human Resources. Richard was told that, although the organization did not have any openings, they were interested in speaking with me.

If nothing else, I'll learn about Human Resource employment opportunities in Pensacola.

February 2001

I feel disconnected and rootless. I'm on a journey with an unknown destination. I seem to have a short-timer's attitude at work because I know I'm moving at some point; I just don't know when. Maybe once we move to Pensacola, get settled, and I find a job, the feeling will dissipate.

We received a gift of dried roses from Heather's funeral. Carol Brown, the wife of my good friend Marcus, came over with their daughter, Alicia, who had shared her magnificent singing voice at Heather's graveside. Unbeknownst to us, they had gathered the flowers for safekeeping. Knowing they would saturate us in a flood of memories, they gave us time to grieve before giving them to us. 'The dried roses were an amazing gift of kindness that meant a lot.

Many years ago, when Heather was a child, one of my uncles explained to her that heather was the name of a plant that grew in Scotland. Captivated by the idea of sharing her name with that small, vibrant purple flower, it carried a special meaning for her. And for us.

A photo in my office reminded me of this. Heather is standing in our yard in her purple scrubs after planting some Heather. The picture and the thought of the plant were so overwhelming, I had to close my office door, close my eyes, and lean my head back.

Although sad, I had an overwhelming sense of her presence in that moment. A Heather Hi. A few minutes later, I felt calm and peaceful. It was as though she tried to calm the raging waters of my discontent and uneasiness about the future.

I think about Heather more often now than when she was alive. Perhaps that speaks to the fact that we often take people and situations for granted. It's like loving the beach but not venturing out to enjoy the sun, sand, and surf when you live in an area with easy access to the beach.

Joyce and I have developed the mindset of not taking things for granted. I just need to let go of my selfishness. I can be resting, exercising, sitting, golfing, working, or writing . . . but no diversion deprives me of thoughts of Heather. In some strange way, maybe this is a blessing. I don't *want* to escape the sense of her presence.

On my way home from a meeting in Huntsville, I listened to a talk about surrender. The speaker indicated that we could pray for what we want, but it may be better to pray for what is best for us—something only God knows.

Dr. Stinnett, a professor at the University of Alabama in Marriage and Family Studies (and someone we attend worship with), asked us to make a presentation to one of his classes about the role grandparents play in raising their grandchildren. Due to a prior commitment, I couldn't attend, but Joyce was able to participate. The invitation confirmed that we were doing the right thing by raising Jakob. Before that class, we had only heard that our decision was wrong. Both our family and conventional wisdom said that it was Donnie's responsibility to raise Jakob.

In the class, Joyce answered questions and shared the perspective of a grandparent caregiver for a grandchild. She went to the class to teach, and God provided her with an overwhelming affirmation of what we were doing.

Both of us have sensed that no matter what else was going on, God was leading us. We just knew we were doing the right thing. Of course, we keep asking ourselves if what we're doing is really the right thing, but we keep coming back to the same answer: *yes*! Although ultimately it may not matter, hearing an expert and students say that we were doing the right thing gave us a real boost.

As I mentioned earlier, Joyce had a successful career in the school system, doing a job she loved. I had retired from the army and found a career that allowed me to work with people I loved. We both anticipated a retirement free of financial worries. The reality is that, despite our commitment to one another, a third party is involved. Scripture talks about a strand of three in a significant relationship. The third strand is God. God's strand is the one that gives us strength when we feel weak and begin to unravel. When we begin to feel tossed about, it's as though God tosses or wraps us in his strand, a lifeline that gets us back on course (Ecclesiastes 4:9–12).

The story of the prodigal son comes to mind because of a skit I helped perform at church (Luke 15:11- 31). I think of Scott as the youngest son and me as the father. In the story of the prodigal son. Jesus tells of a man who divided his inheritance between two sons. Upon receiving his inheritance, the youngest son drifted from home, squandered his portion of the inheritance, and decided he was better off being with his father and went home. The father was ecstatic and welcomed his son with open arms. I have the same hope as the father in the parable, that at some point Scott and I'll be reunited. I feel as though I'm to blame for not paying attention to my son while I'm helping to raise Jakob. I'm also angry with God because of events that seem to be making life so hard: Heather's death, a fire that forced us temporarily to move, being forced to move to Pensacola and give up our lives in Tuscaloosa, having difficulty finding a job in Pensacola (what employer would hire someone who is fifty-three?), Scott becoming more distant—everything! The parable invited me to focus on the father in the story. The father allowed his son to leave. What did the father do as a result? Did he search for his son? What was he doing at home? Did he pray, fret, pace, or did he carry on as if everything were normal? How long had the son been gone?

While we may not have the answers to those questions, we do know the father rejoiced when he was reunited with his son. Playing the role of the father in the skit reminded me of my anger, but it also reminded me of God's constant love, which is the kind of love I need to show toward Scott. The father in the story never gave up loving his son, just as I'll never give up loving my son.

Tom hates that his connection with Scott has been severed, but Leighton helps hold things together.

Will that perseverance pay off? Will I ever lose the feeling that we're in a state of constant transition?

I received another Heather Hi when I found purple flowers growing behind her grave at the cemetery. Again. The entire cemetery seemed like a very gloomy place, except for all those purple flowers and a green patch on her grave. It was just months ago—last November, before heading to a conference in Washington DC—that I had first spotted purple flowers there. The pot of daisy-like flowers that had been tossed against the fence behind Heather's marker. That was the same day I met Carol Cox and Mary Bishop, who were both connected with the human resources community in Pensacola.

The day before I discovered the new array of purple flowers, a flattering email from Carol arrived concerning the résumé I had sent to Landrum HR and the impression it made on the folks at Landrum.

Wow!

March 2001

God is providing answers, and I'm beginning to realize God is patient with me. At times, grief still feels like punishment or a test of faith. God seems to keep pouring it on. For instance, Scott appears excited about the prospect of a job in Dallas. That is so far away, and I fear the miles between us will further distance us from each other. I desperately want him to be close.

Jakob is sick with a viral infection and a very high fever, which will keep us from one of our frequent trips to Fort Walton. It has been some time since Donnie saw Jakob. We were really looking forward to the Thomas Kincaid "Painter of Light" art exhibit in San Destin this weekend, about twenty minutes east of Fort Walton. Because of Jakob's illness, we won't be able to attend. This breaks my heart. Joyce had been anticipating the event, and she feared she would never experience joy again. The very thought of her being so sad made me angry with God. Will we ever experience peace again? This feels like another round of punishment.

We had a special time of prayer at church from 10 p.m. until around midnight. We sang songs, read Scripture, and prayed. A friend offered verses from Job, which made me realize that Job's attitude and fortune improved when he prayed for his friends. He took the focus off himself and looked outward. Although God only restored Job materially, he could still be content because

God would renew relationships with his children in heaven.

Later, Bill Rose, one of the church leaders, said he believed that God had something special in mind for me and that all of this was preparation for those plans.

The next day, Sunday morning worship was as inspiring as the evening prior. The songs we sang, the Scripture we read, and our entire worship touched me. I felt as though the entire congregation was ministering to Joyce and me. Surprisingly, we were not even supposed to be there. We were supposed to be in Fort Walton.

Despite my lack of trust, God must have known we needed to be here. He knew that our concern for Jakob would keep us in Tuscaloosa. Despite our groaning, God knew what was best.

We make plans, and God smiles.

In my attempts to read and pray this morning, I felt particularly thankful for God's friendship. He cares enough to let me rant and rave and be upset. Even though I say hurtful things, he is still there to comfort me and takes it all in. His presence was palpable this morning. He is a friend who will never leave me. He is always there.

Intellectually, I've always known this, but today I felt it. As I prepared to end my quiet time, I felt drawn to reread the passage for March 11 from *Streams in the Desert* by Mrs. Charles Cowen.[3] One statement captivated me: "Sorrow makes deep scars; it writes its record ineffaceably on the heart which suffers." We never get over our griefs; we're never altogether the same after we have passed through them as we were before.

Grief has consumed and incapacitated me. I prayed about it, and God gave me a lesson through that passage. As badly as I

3 Mrs. Charles E. Cowman, *Streams in the Desert: 366 Daily Devotional Readings* (Zondervan, 2006).

feel at times, how much worse off would we be if we did not have God's love? Is it possible that the storm of grief could destroy us emotionally?

Although winds blow and storms come, they will recede, and God will make a path for us to grow stronger and more capable of seeing his will. Our faith holds us fast through the storms of life!

April 2001

I had a job interview with Brit Landrum, the owner of Landrum Human Resources. After the interview, he said they would put a job offer together for me to consider. I was excited. On Tuesday afternoon, I received a call from Yvonne, Senior Human Resources (HR) Manager, offering me a job as an HR manager working under her direction.

After hearing the details of the job, my anger with God resurfaced. Taking the position meant a $10,000 salary cut. It felt like God was jerking me around. God had orchestrated everything else so perfectly, and now, he was going to throw up a money barrier.

Despite the money situation, I liked the quality of the company and the people at Landrum. Based on my limited knowledge of the company, their core values were a good fit for me. Still, I was furious, wondering if we could survive on a lower salary.

God was demanding more than I could deliver. I could not even talk to Joyce about the tremendous sacrifice asked of me. I needed to be alone. So, I wallowed in self-pity for a while, cursing God while cleaning out the bathroom sink.

And then I remembered the people and events that had carried me to this point in time. Meeting Carol and Mary on my way to an HR conference in DC. Carol's connection with Landrum HR. My conversation over dinner with Richard, when he casually mentioned he was having lunch with Mr. Landrum and was willing to pass along a copy of my resume. And then three interviews: first with Mike Perkins, next with Yvonne, and finally, with Mr. Landrum.

Everything had fallen into place perfectly, as though God were guiding me through every step of the hiring process. There were too many coincidences to ignore.

Despite my anger, I asked God to let me know if this was the right job for me.

By the way, despite sending out numerous resumes, I received no other job offers. I started a rejection file much as I had done years ago when I looked for a job after leaving the service. Heather and I had laughed about that.

Moving to Pensacola for a job essentially meant starting over from scratch. From a military career to the HR Director for Northport, Alabama, all the way down to an HR consultant in Pensacola. With the huge salary cut, I felt forced to do something I didn't want to do and give up so much.

Despite my discontent, I kept up a pretty good face at work, but Joyce knew something was wrong. And I kept thinking, *If I'm truly committed to raising Jakob, I have to make sacrifices.* Thinking that way gave me a better perspective on what to do. My biggest hang-up concerned change. Imagine, there I was, a guy who *promoted* change, having *difficulty* with change!

Noah, Abraham, and Moses were plucked out of their everyday lives and had to be content with doing God's bidding, even though they would rather do something else. I empathized with their unhappiness and how they must have grumbled and complained.

After considering the lives of these great men, I'm humbled and feel as though I can do no less.

Joyce said something profound to me, "God put it all together, laid it out, has been directing and leading every step of the way, and now we're going to turn our backs and ignore God's plan?"

Basically, that's like saying, "God, we don't need your help." That would be a real sign of stupidity. We cannot ignore God.

Once I realized that the real problem was my stubbornness and reluctance to make a change, it was easier to accept God's leading. Things seemed to take on a new perspective after that, and peace came with the decision I had to make. Once I recognized that the real problem was *me*, I knew things would work out.

If we follow God's leading, he will take care of us.

May 2001

I think my uncertainty about what to do comes down to the same question: why must the world be this way?"

On May 15th, my *Streams in the Desert* reading focused on trust. I also read some grief literature that referenced Jeremiah 18 for background on trust.

> [1] *This is the word that came to Jeremiah from the LORD:* [2] *"Go down to the potter's house, and there I'll give you my message."* [3] *So I went down to the potter's house, and I saw him working at the wheel.* [4] *But the pot he was shaping from the clay was marred in his hands; so the potter formed it into another pot, shaping it as seemed best to him.*

> [5] *Then the word of the* LORD *came to me.* [6] *He said, "Can I not do with you, Israel, as this potter does?" declares the* LORD. *"Like clay in the hand of the potter, so are you in my hand, Israel.* (Jeremiah 18:1–6).

The end of the Scripture makes it clear that we can trust God to reshape us if necessary.

While at Gateway Church of Christ, we sang the song "Trust and Obey." I reread the lyrics later, and they made an impact. Through different avenues, I'm beginning to get the point; I'm either being taught a lesson, given an answer, or being prepared for something.

June 2001

This Father's Day, I enjoyed reading the cards Heather sent me over the years, as well as the poem she wrote for my fiftieth birthday. The seven-page rhyme is special because that is the sort of thing I wrote for the kids when they were growing up, and Heather reciprocated. Reading this poem might just become an annual Father's Day tradition.

Heather was so young and taken away so soon, without the opportunity to be with her son. Will I ever stop missing her and feeling sad? As strange as it may sound, I don't *want* to stop missing her. Maybe I'm just feeling sorry for myself. Or do I feel sorry for our situation? Our situation must be in God's hands. There is no other way to make sense of any of this without trusting God.

The first card in Heather's handwriting said, "Have a wonderful Father's Day. I wish I could be there, but I'll be thinking of you."

Wow. Talk about a Heather Hi.

It gave me the idea of sending notes to Heather in balloons floating to the sky. It seems appealing, especially if the balloons are sent on special anniversaries like May 27 (her death), June 12 (Father's Day), June 29 (her birthday), July 29 (her wedding anniversary), and December 25. The symbolism is important. Communicating with Heather and sending my notes to heaven is a ritual I'll enjoy.

Today was a gorgeous day with a clear blue sky and the sun filtering through the trees, casting long shadows as it rose. Birds sang, played, and dove into the lake. At one moment, it seemed as though doves were everywhere. I heard them cooing. My thoughts drifted back to Heather, and I couldn't help but miss her. As long as I have both heart and mind, there is no way I can forget her.

It's funny how physical presence means nothing if we have memories. It's kind of like that with Jesus. He is not physically with us, but we know him. Even though we never met the physical Jesus, as we mature, read, listen, and study, we come to know him vividly because of so many reminders through his work, life, and the Father.

The only way to connect or stay in touch with our loved ones is through a memory or spirit state. I'm grateful for my many memories of Heather. Each note I send her in a balloon to heaven will end the same way as my notes to her during her lifetime always ended: "I love you and I'm so proud of you."

July 2001

This month is Heather and Donnie's anniversary. After church, I went to the cemetery and prayed for strength. Almost immediately, a gentle breeze began to flow through the cemetery, and a sense of peace settled over me. That morning, Ecclesiastes 4:9–2 was used in the lesson, the same Scripture used in Donnie's and Heather's wedding ceremony. My prayers focused on receiving affirmation that the decisions we were making were the correct ones.

That feeling of peace may be the affirmation I was seeking.

February 2002

Although it's been a while since I last jotted things down, a lot has happened. We moved to Pensacola, and I began a new job. We're adjusting to a new environment, establishing new friendships, and getting Jakob situated in daycare. Joyce is adjusting to the role of a full-time caregiver. It's safe to say we have been in chaos.

If that wasn't enough, our new church home is in a leadership crisis; the current minister, who had played a significant role in Heather's memorial service, was going to be replaced. We're very disappointed; we thought the church would be our sanctuary.

A visit to the cemetery was special because we saw tiny purple flowers growing near Heather's headstone again.

A Heather Hi day began one morning while the house was still quiet, during my prayer time. An overwhelming sensation struck, and I felt surrounded by God and Heather. The feeling was so incredible that it's hard to describe. I sensed Heather and I worshipping together, feeling as one united with Christ, worshipping in the same dimension. It was a very unusual experience, and when I explained it to Joyce, she cried. Even though I missed Heather's physical presence, joy filled me because we were together in worship.

I continue to pray for understanding of God's will and how all of this is supposed to work together. My experience that morning may have been an answer. It let me know that we're not one-dimensional, and we're not confined to space and time in our relationship with God. We're with each other, always. Physical sight is not essential. Its one-dimensional nature is too confining. I didn't need to see Heather to know she was there, and I want to believe that she was also aware of my presence. Maybe God was giving me the awareness I sought. Later, while reading about leadership and a description of David as a CEO, I came across Psalm 139. Portions of it were among Heather's favorites.

1 You have searched me, LORD,
and you know me.
2 You know when I sit and when I rise;
you perceive my thoughts from afar.
3 You discern my going out and my lying down;
you are familiar with all my ways.
4 Before a word is on my tongue
you, LORD, know it completely.
5 You hem me in behind and before,
and you lay your hand upon me.
6 Such knowledge is too wonderful for me,
too lofty for me to attain.

7 Where can I go from your Spirit?
Where can I flee from your presence?
8 If I go up to the heavens, you are there;
if I make my bed in the depths, you are there.
9 If I rise on the wings of the dawn,
if I settle on the far side of the sea,

[10] even there your hand will guide me,
your right hand will hold me fast.
[11] If I say, "Surely the darkness will hide me
and the light become night around me,"
[12] even the darkness will not be dark to you;
the night will shine like the day,
for darkness is as light to you.

[13] For you created my inmost being;
you knit me together in my mother's womb.
[14] I praise you because I'm fearfully and wonderfully made;
your works are wonderful,
I know that full well.
[15] My frame was not hidden from you
when I was made in the secret place,
when I was woven together in the depths of the earth.
[16] Your eyes saw my unformed body;
all the days ordained for me were written in your book
before one of them came to be.
[17] How precious to me are your thoughts,[a] God!
How vast is the sum of them!
[18] Were I to count them,
they would outnumber the grains of sand—
when I awake, I'm still with you.

October 2002

This past weekend, we visited Tuscaloosa. While we were there, we heard a message from Buddy Bell on Romans 12, specifically verses 1 and 2, reflecting on transformation.

> *Therefore, I urge you, brothers and sisters, in view of God's mercy, to offer your bodies as a living sacrifice, holy and pleasing to God—this is your true and proper worship. Do not conform to the pattern of this world, but be transformed by the renewing of your mind. Then you will be able to test and approve what God's will is—his good, pleasing and perfect will* (Romans 12:1–2).

Joyce and I had just discussed how poorly I was handling everything. Instead of focusing on my relationship with God, I was focusing my anger on Donnie because we had given up so much to move to Pensacola.

It has been three years and five months since the accident. UNBELIEVEABLE! Not a day goes by that I don't think of Heather. I feel as connected to her today as always. In some ways, I feel closer. I love that feeling. It brings me closer to God because I know she is with God.

I don't cry as often as I used to, but that does not diminish the depth of my grief. Does time really heal wounds? Paul had a thorn in the flesh that he carried with him. Grief is kind of like a thorn buried too deep to pull out. It will always be with us. Although it hurts like hell, removing it would be like giving up the time we did have with Heather. That's the only way grief won't hurt.

For now, I'll enjoy the present and be grateful for the time we have with Jakob. As we build our relationship with Jakob, it may become difficult for Donnie because we spend more time with Jakob than he does and have more input into the decisions shaping Jacob's life. It must be God's will, and I need to understand that.

Jakob is a blessing. I need to be more accepting of the blessing and live gratefully in the present instead of wondering, "what if."

November 2002

Sometimes I feel very impatient with my visitor, grief, even though he is here to stay. I'm ready to move on and do something else, but I can't, because he stays with me, slowing me down—just like a thorn in my side. I'm anxious to see things improve, at least to my standards of "better." Metaphorically, I'd like to see a blue sky again, but there is a filter that prevents the blue from showing through. Perhaps it's like waiting for a bus that never arrives. I can't go anywhere without transportation!

There is a void without Heather. I think of the games we played, the trips we took, our conversations, breakfasts together, shopping, watching her with Jakob, and hearing her play the piano. Those precious moments are gone, and I'll have to fill time with something else: Jakob, work, church, and just nonsense.

And Tom and Heather worked puzzles together.

July 2003

While on the way to work, listening to the radio, a female voice sang "Going Home" from Dvořák's New World Symphony. Powerful! I can only think that it is well with my soul. Joyce sent me a short clipping about an old guy who had begun mentoring a young, fatherless boy. Reminds me of my relationship with Jakob.

I received a call from Mike Shaw, the superintendent of water systems for Northport. I hadn't spoken with him in years. He had recently attended a graveside funeral for Ricky Harrison. He was buried close to Heather's grave, and it reminded him of me. He wanted me to know how much he and others missed me. His words made me feel pretty good. I have the overwhelming feeling of being protected and surrounded.

August 2003

One night, while praying over Jakob, I saw Heather's picture and lamented about how much I missed her, and, of course, I cried.

On the way to church the next morning to set up the audiovisual equipment for worship, I tuned in to a radio station I usually don't listen to and heard, "Go Rest High on the Mountain." Scott had read those lyrics as a poem at Heather's graveside ceremony. Even more serendipitous, the song played as we drove across the three-mile bridge on the way to church—the same route Heather took every day on her way to Sacred Heart. She told us how she would exclaim how pretty it was and wondered how anyone could doubt that there was a God.

Another Heather Hi.

OCTOBER 7, 2003

Joyce and Jakob came along for the ride when I attended a conference in Orlando, and on the way back to Pensacola, we picked up my mom, whom we call Grandma Gert, so that she could spend a couple of days with us. When we got home, Joyce suggested that Mom and Jakob play a card game called Trouble. After a few moments, Mom quit.

"Jakob's cheating," she said. "No matter how old he is, there is no excuse for cheating."

Jakob was concerned about being in trouble. "Maybe she just doesn't understand the game," he said to Joyce.

"Grandma Gert is having memory problems," Joyce explained. "Her mind isn't as sharp as it once was."

"Oh. Okay," Jakob said. "We can play it her way."

For me, this was a Heather Hi because that is exactly how Jakob's mom would have responded. Rather than being combative, she would be the peacemaker.

Although a lot has happened since the last journal entry, I was so concerned with being successful in a new career and being a good role model for Jakob that it never crossed my mind to continue writing.

Personal Stories

Countless friends and family have surrounded our family since Heather's passing, and there may be value in having key people share their observations and feelings about her. The following storytellers, except Angela, Scott's wife, were part of Heather's life as family members, relatives, or friends. We all witnessed her mature into a woman of dignity and grace. Her child, Jakob/Jamie, and niece, Leighton, only know her through these stories.

In sharing them with you, I hope to illustrate how the grief brought on by one person's passing can prompt reflections that ultimately deepen the value we place on our relationships—particularly those shaped by shared experiences and lasting memories.

Tom: Father

The author of this book, Tom, is a devoted father shaped by discipline, duty, and deep reflection. He brings a lifetime of varied experiences to his journey through grief. His bond with Heather was unshakable—a relationship marked by admiration, gentleness, and pride. In telling his own story here, and sharing his journal entries in the previous pages, he invites us into the heart of a father's love and the depth of his loss.

You need to understand a little bit about me and how I grew up so that my approach to living with grief makes sense. I love privacy and spending time alone to reflect and contemplate. I have an active imagination. I can be spontaneous too, except when attending meetings, because I like to know the purpose ahead of time. I'm comfortable acting before having all the details, and I often jump in, ready to improvise and adapt to the situation. I can be stubborn at times and often too demanding of others.

I'm the son of Naomi Gertrude, a southern belle, and Raymond Aubrey, a career army officer; the brother of Randy and Terry (identical twins); and Denise. Our family was blessed with lots of fun, travel, and adventure. My brothers and I often reflect on memories of our formative years, and we still manage to get together at least twice a year to golf.

If I were to plot my life on a line where one dot marks birth and another dot marks death, there is a lot of space. In that space, many events took place that formed and continue to shape my character. (I hope to complete this character-building adventure in writing before the last dot on that line.)

While growing up, my brothers and I participated in a wide range of activities, including Boy Scouts, camping, hiking, and sports. We spent most of our days outdoors. We also found time to terrorize our younger sister, Denise, and managed to push Mom's buttons. We were slow to recognize that pushing Mom's buttons would not have a favorable outcome for us. Whenever we went too far, she called upon dad to discipline us.

Although Dad was a quiet man, he was very capable of corralling his sons and using his discretionary power as a parent to bring the hammer down. In addition to disciplining, he taught us the values of teamwork, self-reliance, and problem-solving. If we had an issue, he expected us to come up with a solution. He instilled in us the idea that real men don't cry.

Dad was an army lieutenant colonel and a veteran of World War II and Vietnam. He believed in exposing our family to as many experiences and cultures as possible; therefore, when he came up for reassignment, he took us with him.

Dad did not outwardly display emotion. I only recall a couple of times when I saw him angry. Mom, on the other hand, frequently exposed my brothers and me to her anger.

After meeting Joyce, Dad was so impressed that he told me I should not let her get away. When she said "yes," I thought I'd won the lottery. Dad knew she was smarter than me. She graduated with honors in English in three and a half years and began her teaching career. I completed my college career in four and a half years and received a commission as a second lieutenant through the Army Reserve Officers' Training Corps (ROTC). Dad was proud of me for completing Airborne, Ranger, and rotary wing flight training, as well as my early successes as a young officer.

Accepting all challenges, being self-reliant, and doing everything I could to ensure my survival during various assignments consumed me. Showing any form of weakness was unacceptable.

I became infatuated with the name Heather long before Joyce and I met. A married couple I befriended in college would often invite me over, and we listened to an album featuring a song titled "Heather."[4] After hearing that song, I decided that

---

4 Tony Sandler and Ralph Young, *Pretty Things Come in Twos* (ABC Records, 1973), vinyl.

if I ever had a daughter, I would name her Heather. My plan was nonnegotiable.

I thought the name Heather was unique and gave it no more thought. Then I discovered that heather is a flower native to Scotland, displaying purple, white, or pink flowers. Purple, as you may have noticed, was Heather's favorite color. But there is more to her name than that. According to Celtic mythology, a child named Heather is believed to embody values of gracefulness, loyalty, and kindness. These qualities perfectly describe my daughter.

Whenever we moved into a new home, we always planted heather plants. They manage to flourish.

Heather has been part of most of my adult life. Even in her absence, she is still a significant pattern in its fabric. Though I may pretend to be stoic, I'll always have a soft spot for her. As Joyce will tell you, in my eyes, Heather could do no wrong. She was a great kid who gave us very few problems. Even mentioning that I was disappointed in her would break her heart, and rarely was further action needed.

Heather loved animals, and they seemed to love her in return, and not just dogs and cats. I always found it fascinating to see wild ducks perched near her in our backyard. She had an indescribably sweet spirit, and I don't think there was a malicious bone in her body, for she did everything within her power to avoid chaotic situations and often told me that she did not understand how people could be so mean. In her role as a pediatric nurse, she was infuriated to see children arrive at the hospital with obvious signs of abuse.

We all have different histories and come from various family cultures, so our approach to dealing with whatever life throws at us is different too. My brothers, sister, and I have lost both parents, yet the only common denominator is loss. We each dealt with their deaths differently, and yet we were in the same family. I'm the only sibling who has lost a child, so I have experienced a different kind of grief than my brothers and sister.

The influences of my family life, the army, my professional careers, education, training, and life experiences have shaped the way I meet challenges. Yet, none of those influences prepared me for the event that would change me completely and forever.

Whenever I think I have contained my grief, it rises like a jack-in-the-box without warning. When I put it back in the box, I know it will undoubtedly pop up again without warning.

Letter to Heather for Her Wedding Day

July 27, 1995

Dear Princess,

Your daddy remembers. No one can understand how it feels to relinquish the nurturing of your daughter to another man. In my opinion, no one can do it as well as I. I'm excited while being sad. I'm excited for you and Donnie B, and for the life you're beginning together as one. I'm saddened because my job is over. The closest comparison I can think of is preparing for a major military exercise. All the work, training, and preparation that goes into it is mind-boggling. Then it happens. Then it's over. Then what? I've spent your entire life so far being your daddy, and that will continue, but from now on, my role will be different. While that is exciting and will present new challenges, I'll miss my little girl. I keep thinking about the memories and the speed with which the events of our lives unfold. Thank goodness for videos so that we can look back and remember.

I remember clearly where I was and what I was doing when you were born, and even before that, I vividly recall being in Airborne school at Fort Benning, Georgia, with your mom pregnant. Better yet, I remember your conception.

I still see you on my shoulders at Cowhouse Creek in Ft Hood, Texas. I hear you learning to say *helicopter* at Mineral Wells, Texas, and see you holding your breath until you pass out. I'll never forget the little girl who stood in the window and waved bye-bye at our quarters at Ft Lewis, Washington, or our experience of toting you up the side of Mt Ranier and having you drool down my cheek. Can you remember our trip to Yuma, Arizona? We sang and made cassette tapes along the way, and you fell into the pool while I swam. Boy, was Mom mad when I brought you to the apartment, soaking wet.

I recall how I looked forward to buying gifts for you and Scott while I was in Korea. I remember you riding a Big Wheel, with short hair, attending piano recitals, wrapping Christmas gifts, and undergoing a splenectomy. That memory still hurts; we almost lost you. Do you remember your first camp at Camp Wiregrass near Enterprise, Alabama? I went out every night to check on you. That was probably more for my benefit than yours.

Sledding, skiing, traveling, and retreats in Berchtesgaden, Germany, along with our trip to Paris with you and Scott, are just a few highlights of my tour of duty in Germany. Don't forget our trip to London, the sad loss of your hamster, our quarters at Camp King near Frankfurt, the swim team competition, and missing the debut of the movie *E.T.* because you were on restriction. Wow! Lots of opportunities to bond.

When did I realize you were growing into a woman? If I had realized it, I don't think I would have accepted it.

We moved back to the States for an assignment at the University of Alabama in Tuscaloosa, and you began your high school career. You and Mary Ann became best friends as you learned to drive. (There is no doubt you can back a car better than anyone. Remember, I told you that backing is a different skill set than moving forward.) Playing the flute in the high school band, marching during football games, and singing in the chorus. Remember our red, green, and yellow code when you're at a party or on a date. I'll never forget being trapped in the attic just outside your room, and my cries for help being ignored. One of my favorite memories was our weekly visits to the City Café in Northport for breakfast.

Next on the timeline are your years at Harding University in Arkansas. Sadness, homesickness, Spring Sing performance, and the utterly ridiculous cows, B Rock Overlook, Little Rock, your roommate Melanie (who was another best friend), and, of course, Donnie B., I know you will never forget the fun you had and the great work you did for a small church in Griffithville, Arkansas, nor how Operation Desert Storm derailed your opportunity to study abroad. I was so proud of the choices you made. There is so much more, and I could go on and on, but enough is enough. Suddenly, we're making wedding plans. I felt like chopped liver since you and Mom had everything under control.

It was only twenty-five years ago that it all began when your mother and I committed our relationship, a relationship we continue to build upon. I'm proud to be your dad for life and gratefully accept the honor God has bestowed upon me. I look forward to watching you and Donnie grow in your commitment to each other and God.

Loving father of the bride,
Daddy

Heather's Letter to Her Father

July 29, 1995

Dear Dad,

I wanted to get both you and Mom a card that expressed exactly what I'm feeling and thinking at this moment in my life, and that told how much I love and appreciate you. I found a card for the mother of the bride, but they don't make them for the father of the bride. I know because I looked everywhere. So, I decided to write a note instead.

I loved the letter you gave me! It was perfect. It made me laugh and cry. It's funny how just one word or a couple of words bring back a flood of memories. I can't believe you remembered all that. I guess you remember more than we give you credit for. That letter is so special to me, and I know that I'll love reading it over and over.

I want you to know how much I enjoyed these last weeks of being at home and spending time with you and Mom. It's been a really special time, and it's been a lot of fun. As always, you have kept everyone from getting nervous and uptight with your jokes and sense of humor. One of the things I love about our family is our ability to laugh together. There has never been a shortage of laughter in our home. You have taught me the importance of laughter and humor in a family, and that it's okay to laugh at yourself (which you do regularly). I hope Donnie and I'll be able to carry that into our own family.

It has been so hard to put into words what I'm feeling on my wedding day. There is such a mixture of feelings and emotions. I'm so excited to be marrying Donnie. I have no doubt about my love for him or his for me. Yet, at the same time, I'm sad because a chapter of my life is about to be over. (This marriage thing is going to take some getting used to.) There is still a part of me that wants to be a little girl and have my mom and dad take care of me. But I don't suppose that would be normal, and people might think that we were weird. Well, I guess some people think that already. One of the hardest things for me to get used to is going to be depending on Donnie for most of the things I have always depended on you for. Things like hanging ceiling fans or picture frames, problems with my car, any kind of problem, be it spiritual, emotional, or otherwise. But I'll always be your little girl, and I'll always depend on you to make me laugh until we cry, to cheer me up (you can do that better than anyone), to let me beat you at Rumikubs, to be the spiritual person that I look up to more than anyone, and to be my dad—the best in the world.

I learned so much from you and your life and marriage. I learned to be honest and to do what I say I'm going to do. I learned never to give up. I learned that patience is a virtue. I learned that it's okay to laugh and cry. I learned that your family comes first. I learned the importance of friendships. I learned how to love another person. I learned about God and how to have a relationship with Him.

You taught me so much by your example and how to live your life. God blessed me so much with you and Mom, and I thank Him every night for you.

I really must close this out, or I'll be crying uncontrollably. I love you so much, and this day is going to be so special. Thank you for making it special and for always being my dad.

Your Princess,

Heather

Joyce: Mother

Despite her grief, Joyce poured herself into being the best mother figure she could be for her grandchild, hoping that Jakob, now Jamie, would not suffer because of losing one parent. After raising two children, Joyce knew firsthand the drama that comes with navigating the different and challenging stages of their lives. With Jamie, she once again became the epitome of what it means to nurture a child.

Learning to live with a broken heart is a chaotic and exhausting journey that no one wants to undertake when a part of yourself is missing. Nothing in my fifty years of life had prepared me for the phone call that turned my world upside down.

Before that phone call, my life had been peaceful and happy—not perfect, but a life I could call a dream come true. I grew up in a small rural community with loving parents and four older sisters. I attended college, earned a degree in education, and married the love of my life. Although I taught school for a few years, I intended to become a wife and mother; that's what I became. We had two beautiful children, Heather and Scott. They were the center of my life.

Tom and I loved being parents and were happy watching them grow into successful adults. Heather became a nurse and was truly my best friend. As she entered her professional world, we spoke on the phone daily, and she shared her life with me. After a six-week medical mission trip to Africa, she told me that she thought she would like to return for a more extended period of two years. I was glad that didn't happen. In those days, before cell phones, email, and video calls were available, I couldn't imagine her being away for that long.

Instead of going on another mission trip, she married the love of *her* life, and she and Donnie gave us our first grandchild. Again, my life was fulfilling all my dreams.

Heather was only twenty-seven years old, and she had a nine-month-old baby when the call came that she had died instantly in an automobile accident. The shock of that call is indescribable. The following days were consumed by the deepest pain I had ever known. My niece, Debbie, was there to hold me up and plan a celebration of life ceremony. In the midst of everything, there was a baby to care for.

But I also wanted to die. I begged God to please let me die to escape the pain. I couldn't live through the experience—and living is not the way I would describe the next few years. I merely existed. All my energy was poured into taking care of Jakob (a.k.a. Jamie). People said I was so blessed to have Heather's child in my life. I was and still am, but those first years brought as much heartache as happiness. Those first steps, first words, first days of kindergarten—and all the other milestones—were reminders that Heather wasn't around to experience them.

The year of this writing, 2024, marks the twenty-fifth anniversary of Heather's death. I'm reminded that I couldn't bear the idea of her spending two years in Africa. How much simpler *that* would have been.

Looking back, I recognize so many people who played significant roles along the way. Tom and I stumbled through rocky terrain, but the long journey of grief has cemented our love and devotion to each other. In those early weeks, when I hid in a closet to weep, he found me and said, "Don't ever hide your tears from me." He held me in his arms, and we cried together.

My sister, Bobbie, called me every day just as Heather had done. At first, I couldn't even talk to her, but she always called to listen to me cry and say, "I love you" over and over.

Heather's best friend, Mary Ann, became another daughter to us. For twenty-five years, she has never wavered in her love and friendship. All those years, she has found time in her busy life as a wife, mother, and nurse to travel and spend time with us.

Our lives will never be the same. There was our life before fifty and our life after fifty. We came to think of ourselves as amputees: we continue living but with a vital part missing. I have had faith in God since I was a small child, but that faith wavered as I struggled with the "why" questions. A deeper faith than I ever could have imagined has replaced my childlike faith. I found no answers to why, but I have been able to let go of the questions. I'm so grateful to have had twenty-seven years with our precious Heather and thankful to have her child as an essential part of my life. Memories of Heather sustain me now, but there is never a day that I don't think of her and miss her.

One of my greatest regrets of my grief journey is that I failed as a mom to my son. I "took care" of my kids, but during those dark days, I couldn't take care of Scott. I didn't know how to help him in his grief journey over the loss of his sister. I wasn't there for him as I had always been. In a role reversal, he became my rock. He held me up when I needed it most and continues to do so today.

Shortly after Scott's daughter was born, he held me in his arms, crying, and asked, "How did you survive the death of your child?"

It's a pain too deep for words; it's living with a broken heart.

Letter from Joyce

June 29, 2009

My sweet Heather,

It's time to say goodbye. It has taken so long. At this cemetery, I watched your body being buried in the ground. But I couldn't let you go, so I just let myself die, and for ten years, I have tried to live your life for you. I have given Jakob as much love as I could give him since you died, and I'll continue to do that forever because he is a part of you—for nine months while you were here with him, you told him so many times, "I love you more than life itself." I always wondered why you chose that phrase, but there is no doubt that you poured your heart of love into that precious baby, and it remains there. No one can replace a "Mother's love"—I cannot do that for Jakob, but I believe I have given him the security of knowing that others love him, and that's the best I can do.

For so long, I kept myself buried in your life here, or what I saw as your life, but you are not here. You are in your eternal home, shouting at me, "Mom, don't worry about me."

I'm sorry it's taken so long for me to hear you. Your "little brother," Scott, has been instrumental in making me hear you. Several weeks ago, he told me I *had* to listen to "Sissy's Song" by Alan Jackson, and though I have heard it at least twenty-five times over the past week, the one phrase that I knew *you* were saying to *me* was, "Don't worry 'bout me."

I'm going to say goodbye to you today when I leave the cemetery; no, not goodbye to my love for you, not goodbye to the wonderful twenty-seven-plus years of memories of the life blessed with so much happiness, not goodbye to your precious child. But I'm saying goodbye to my efforts to live your life on your behalf. I'm not sure what my life is supposed to be, but you know that ranger dad of yours can find the right path for us. Now that he will have his wife back, perhaps it will be easier for him to see himself again. Maybe it will be through continuing to raise Jakob, or perhaps not. I'm leaving that in God's hands to do what is best for Jakob. I surrendered Jakob to God when he was two years old, but God gave him back to us.

I realize now that God didn't mean for me to be "you," nor to step into Donnie's life. I was to be the surrogate mom and Jakob's primary caregiver for as long as Jakob needed me. I can continue in that role now if that's where God places Jakob again; I understand my role now. I'll be me, living *my* life with whatever direction God wants me to take.

I'm going now to spend just a few minutes with you and leave some flowers and seashells at your grave. And then I'll say goodbye. I know I'll hear you saying, "Tell Dad I love him," like you did every time we talked on the phone when Dad wasn't at home. And I'll do just that! As I set you free, thank you for setting me free.

See you soon—
Mom

Scott: Brother

Scott, Heather's brother, married his true love, Angela, and together they raise their daughter, Leighton, who is the apple of Scott's eye. He will gladly tell you that Heather was the "wind beneath his wings."

Mother and daughter celebrating the wedding.

Scott and his big little sister

Even though she was maybe 5'4" and 115 pounds, and I stood at 6'3" and 250 pounds, I was always her "little brother," and this was how she always introduced me.

That phrase usually produced a laugh, which is a good way to try to describe our relationship—laughter, jokes, pranks, often sarcasm, but one that was full of "known" love. "Known" love because it wasn't said often enough between a brother and a sister, but I have no doubt Heather loved me and knew I loved her. The last words I said to Heather were, "I love ya, sis, and can't wait to see you next week."

That week never happened.

To say my life changed in a moment is true, but that seems too small, too finite a statement to encompass the effect, the continued effect, it has on me. See, she was my "big sis," but she was also the person who talked me through big decisions, got me to talk about my feelings, counseled me on girls, and kept me out of trouble. Looking back, one of the most important things she did was to work as a liaison (for lack of a better term) between me and my parents. She tried (mostly successfully) to keep the peace, educated me on how to speak out or ask for things, and reminded me to call mom and dad on birthdays and anniversaries.

See, my sister had the most incredible relationship with my parents, and then she was gone. I was devastated, and the person I usually talked to about these things, who helped me communicate with my parents, was no longer there. My relationship with them suffered.

In my mind, my sis was the "good" child, and now I was lost. I needed to fill some of the void she left. This task was so daunting that I basically chose not to deal with it. Physically, I lost my sister, but, for a time, I also lost my parents. Due to my fear of not being able to be what they needed me to be, and not having the person I usually would talk to about this, I chose not to heal. Not sure which stage of the grief model that falls under, but I know I stayed there for a long time.

My relationship with my parents has grown over the years, and I now feel closer to them than I ever have. This is because they worked through their "grief stages" and emotions more than I did. Admittedly, I've blocked out much of what I should have dealt with, which is why writing my personal story, a task my dad assigned to me, has been difficult. Twenty-five years later, there are still things that I have never dealt with and need to. Maybe, as Tim McGraw sings, "In my next thirty years."

As time passes and my thoughts, feelings, and perspectives change, I find myself thinking of my sister more often, wishing she could meet my wife and my daughter, her niece. I imagine her relationship with them, the advice she would give me, and the laughter we would all share. Talking about Heather now typically brings a smile to my heart, as I share her with my wife and daughter, but I still don't let myself delve too deeply, choosing not to confront some thoughts and emotions. Maybe I'll one day. Maybe I'll try to be like my dad and write a book.

Heather's death has left so many questions—what ifs, what might-have-beens—that it still overwhelms me. That's why I chose not to focus on the past. For the most part, this task has asked me to focus on the past.

Is this right? Wrong? Is there a right or a wrong way to deal with my loss, to cope? I'm not a smart or deep enough thinker to go there.

What I do know is I love my "big sis," and I'm thankful for my memories of her:

- How she could talk so fast, my parents had no idea what she was saying.
- How quickly her little feet could fly up and down the stairs in our house.
- How great she was at putting the angel on top of the Christmas tree.

A tradition that continues with Scott and Leighton.

- All the times we fell getting off the ski lift.
- The cold water she dumped on me in the shower (I got her back).
- Helping me dress in junior high and high school so I'd be "cool."

I'm thankful I got to be her "little" brother.

I hope I'm making her proud.

Donnie & Jamie: Husband & Child

Husband and child

Jamie and her father are very close. They enjoy spending time together, whether snow skiing, attending sporting events, concerts, or music festivals. Jamie loves to hear stories about how her father and Heather met at Harding University in Arkansas.

Father and son hanging out.

Heather studied nursing at Harding; Donnie studied business. They met at a school-sponsored event in May of 1994. When not in school, Donnie worked with his father in his father's construction company, Barber Construction Inc., in Fort Walton Beach. The things Donnie can do with a piece of land are remarkable!

When Heather and Donnie first met, Joyce and I weren't sure about the nature of their relationship. If we asked Heather about Donnie, she would say there wasn't any chemistry, whatever that means. But even though Donnie graduated three years ahead of Heather, they stayed in touch after Donnie graduated. Fast forward to July 29, 1995, and they were married.

Once married, they moved to Navarre, Florida, and Heather worked as a pediatric nurse at Sacred Heart Hospital in Pensacola, while Donnie continued working with his father at Barber Construction. Then, on August 18, 1998, Jakob (now known as Jamie) was born.

Donnie and Jamie share in the grief of losing a wife and mother, but they experience their grief differently.

Donnie's grief made me think of a storm response.

Living on the Gulf Coast presents special challenges during hurricane season. Donnie's construction acumen and his ability to perform magic with a piece of dirt resulted in frequent calls for help with storm recovery. As a builder, Donnie was used to handling physical property damage, and he could fix anything. Yet all his skills and knowledge could not prepare him for the storm of grief over Heather's death. Grief's storm created a different kind of damage.

About the time Donnie thought he had grief under control and was ready to move on, overwhelming sorrow would stop him in his tracks, and for a period, he would become incapacitated. Things would improve until another storm rolled in. Despite Donnie's strong faith, endless questions arose. Was God as good as Donnie had been taught to believe? Where was God? Why didn't God stop the accident from happening? Why did Jamie survive, but Heather didn't?

Jamie's own story is very different from her father's. Jamie cannot recall a time when she was aware of her mom. After all, she was only nine months old when Heather died. So, while she may not be aware of Heather's physical presence, she sees the effects of Heather's life on many of the people she grew up around.

Joyce and I tried to help our grandchild get to know her mother by talking about Heather a lot—her likes and dislikes, the travels our family took when Heather and Scott were growing up, Heather's adventures after she set out on her own, her integrity, and her strong sense of right and wrong. It wasn't beyond Heather to go toe-to-toe with doctors when they prescribed the wrong medicine or to feel furious when a child came into the hospital with obvious physical abuse.

Jamie's experience of grief was different. As a baby, Jamie would have felt her mother's absence without having the language or memory to hold it the same way adults do. By sharing stories with Jamie about Heather, Jamie could sense something about who her mother was and clearly see how Heather's death affected Donnie and us.

Jamie tells us she always felt something was missing from her young life. She missed having a mom. She felt left out when she saw other kids' moms pick them up from school or participate in school events. Through the stories our family shared, she had the opportunity to get to know her mom.

She says that experiencing the sense of loss and the accompanying grief taught her several things.

1. Don't take family or anyone for granted because you never know how long you're going to have them.
2. Cherish every moment you can spend with your beloved family and friends.
3. Treat others as if it were going to be the last time you will see them.
4. Never leave a situation or relationship on a negative note.

Jamie attempts to live a regret-free life by following these principles.

Heather's Prayer for Her Child

I pray that you will always be as sweet as you are right now. I pray that you will grow up to be healthy and strong, that you will like sports and playing outside, that you will love your family and enjoy spending time with us, that you will grow up to be confident in yourself and independent, and that you will love people and serve others. Most of all, I pray that you will grow to have a lasting relationship with your Lord and Savior and that you will serve Him your entire life.

Angela: Sister-in-Law

Angela came into Tom, Joyce, and Donnie's lives after their journey with grief began. As Scott's girlfriend and now wife, she has adapted to being a bonus mom to Scott's daughter, Leighton, and is teaching her to be a woman of integrity.

Grief. It washes over people in different ways at various times. In the beginning, a tsunami strikes, leaving a path of destruction that reshapes the landscape. While I wasn't around for the initial hit, my husband, Scott, shared with me how he felt when he first learned of his sister's death. It was a moment that brought him to his knees and left him submerged in a sea of doubt. He questioned everything he had ever believed in.

By the time I became a part of Scott's life, at least ten years had passed since Heather's accident. Her memory trickled in here and there throughout the year and swelled into tumultuous

Another family growing together.

waves in May, June, July, and then in August—all calendar reminders of her death, birthday, anniversary, and Jakob's birth. Every one of these emotional moments gave us a reason to talk about Heather.

I know from Scott's stories that Heather poured her sweet spirit into other people. I know that, as tiny as she was, she could make Scott listen to her. So many times, he told me, "I wish that you two could have met each other. She would have helped you understand me."

Scott misses his sister, but the pain of her absence is most evident on holidays. He wanted so much to make Heather's spirit a part of our Christmas celebrations. He would hold Leighton on his shoulders to put the angel on the top of the Christmas tree, just like Heather used to do. We made Heather's recipes—Cypress Inn muffins, green bean casserole, and Georgia carrots. While I know that these actions do not erase her absence, they allow me and Hope—Leighton's middle name, and the one she prefers—to share in her memory, even though we never knew her.

I'm not sure if Heather's loss motivated Scott's love for life, but he tries to capture every moment of happiness while he can. He loves deeply and always shows it through acts of service. He is the best husband and father I could ask for, and I know his big sister is so proud of him.

Debbie: Cousin

Debbie's bond with Heather began even before Heather was born. As a teenager, she was especially close to her Aunt Joyce, Heather's mother, and treasured the time they spent together during Joyce's pregnancy. From those early days of anticipation, Debbie's connection with Heather grew—nurtured by letters, family visits, and years marked by both deep love and heartbreaking loss.

Joyce with niece Debbie. They are so close.

I was a freshman in high school when Heather was born. Her mom, my Aunt Joyce, came to our house a few days before her birth because we were closer to a military hospital. Her dad, Uncle Tom, was on an assignment in the desert somewhere, leading up to her due date. I was thrilled to spend this time with Aunt Joyce, as she was like a big sister to me, whom I truly idolized. What fun I had with her walking each evening, guessing if this was a boy or a girl baby, and if this twitch or pain could be the start of labor. It wasn't long before I came home from school to hear the news that the baby was a girl, and her name was Heather! Thus began my journey with her.

Through the early years of her life, I only knew of Heather through Aunt Joyce's letters, pictures, and at least yearly visits from their multiple military stations. As a kindergartner, Heather and her baby brother Scott lived at my grandmother's house while Tom was in Korea for fifteen months. I remember visiting them and thinking Heather was one of the sweetest, prettiest five-year-olds I had ever known. When I was married, Aunt Joyce was my Matron of Honor, and Heather, with two other cousins dressed in matching dresses, passed out rice bags at our reception. I was so blessed to have Heather's family living just forty-five minutes away during my first year of marriage. As college students, my husband and I spent many Friday nights eating dinner with them and playing Candyland with Heather and Scott.

Then they were off to Germany, and again Aunt Joyce kept me up to date on Heather's escapades as a preteen. I had a daughter of my own, and I spent many times on the phone asking mother-type questions of her. We even made a brief visit to Germany with our baby, Lauren, where Heather played with her like a doll!

When Heather was in high school, we lived only an hour away again. As my husband and I traveled on business trips, Heather would come and babysit. Then she headed to college, and I was so proud to hear she was studying nursing – it fit her caring, loving personality. She traveled to Africa on a medical mission trip, and I remember thinking she was so ahead of me spiritually, such a mature Christian young woman. After graduating from college, Heather's first job was in our current home city of Birmingham, Alabama, and I asked her to live with us as she got settled. Looking back now, I treasure these days so much. She was so busy as a young neonatal nurse, but she would come and sit in my kitchen and share her day with me. We talked of work, books, love for God, and, of course, young men. We moved away before Heather married the love of her life. Once again, I was kept up to date on Heather's life through Aunt Joyce. All of us rejoiced at the birth of Heather's baby, Jakob!

Then our joy turned to sorrow on May 27, 1999. I can't think of the phone call telling me of her death without feeling my stomach knot. From that day to now, I still have thoughts of "Why Heather?" I rushed to my beloved aunt and uncle's side, grappling with what to say, how to help, and wanting so desperately to make it better. But on that day, we all changed. Things that were fun as a family lost their fun. Some traditions were tried and dropped. Years went by before I could talk to Aunt Joyce about a book, because my English teacher aunt could not make herself read. It was hard to share things about my daughter with them at times, because she has lived long past Heather's life span now. We're all in that grip of grief that I don't believe will go away until we're reunited with Heather in heaven.

What do we do with this grief? Some try to stuff it, not talk about it, and avoid mentioning Heather's name. I'm sure I have done this at times, but Joyce and Tom have taught me to talk about Heather. I have glimmers of Heather at times—sure she would have been there, done this, said that—and I love sharing these moments with them, and they share their Heather Hi's with me.

Over the years, I've tried many ways to honor Heather, my aunt, and uncle. Right after the funeral, my daughter and son gathered their teen bands and held a benefit concert for a scholarship fund for Jakob. I had Jakob visit me with Aunt Joyce in the summers. We lit candles for Heather at family gatherings. When my husband and I had the funds, we started a nursing scholarship in Heather's honor. For several years, it was our tradition to spend Memorial Day Weekend (the weekend of Heather's death) at the beach with Aunt Joyce and Uncle Tom. Since my divorce, a nursing award has been established to honor one student who embodies the qualities we all admired in Heather. We travel to the nursing pinning ceremony and present this award each year.

Does any of this "fix our grief"? No. As a matter of fact, some years are more awkward than others as we try to be there for each other. Heather has become a saint of sorts to me. I have been blessed by having the recipe for Cypress Inn muffins shared with me, which were some of Heather's favorites. Eating them brings on a flood of pleasant memories. I'm so grateful to her parents for showing me how to keep going through tremendous loss and pain.

Mary Ann: Best Friend

This tribute comes from Heather's best friend in junior high and high school—someone who found in Heather the answer to a heartfelt prayer for a faithful companion. Their bond took root through shared faith, notes passed between classes, and the everyday joys of growing up together.

Best friends forever and always.

"BFF" and the day of the week. That is what we wrote on our handwritten notes before meticulously folding them into neat, origami-type squares with a tab that you could pull to open. We passed them to each other in the hallway during class change or poked them through the little vent on our lockers. We wrote notes planning what we would do that weekend and what we would wear. We wrote about the boys we liked, the ones we thought were "fine."

Heather and I shared what was on our hearts in those notes and also encouraged each other: "Good luck on the Algebra test," "Love your outfit today."

This was our approach to texting in the 1980s, way before cell phones and social media.

I met Heather at Riverside Junior High School. We were both in ninth grade. She had just moved to Tuscaloosa, Alabama, from Germany. Before I met her, I felt lonely and longed for a best friend. Don't get me wrong, I had friends. I just wanted one special, close friend.

As a born-again Christian, I had a strong faith. Raised in the Southern Baptist tradition, I was very active in my church. How it all happened is a "God-thing." Heather and I both played the flute. I remember looking up one day in band class, and it was like God said, "There she is. She will be your best friend."

We started talking and found out we had so much in common. Our friendship was easy, effortless. We just genuinely loved spending time together, being silly teenage girls.

We spent the following summer together. We went to the beach, the pool, on youth trips, and to band camp. During this time, I pretty much became part of the Knox family. Their home was warm, secure, and full of laughter and fun. I just love them and would always feel accepted and loved in their home.

Heather and I walked into Tuscaloosa County High School in 1986 as frightened tenth graders and walked out in May of 1989 as confident high school graduates. The years in between were some of the happiest years of my life. So many firsts happened during that time, and I know those years would not have been the same without my best friend, Heather.

The Many Attributes of Heather

Heather was compassionate. Heather was probably one of the sweetest people you could ever meet. She would give the most thoughtful gifts and write such encouraging notes, letters, and cards.

The movie Beaches was released in theaters in the 1980s. We saw it together. It was a movie about friendship. (If you want a good cry, I totally recommend this movie.) Bette Midler was one of the actresses and sang the theme song, "Wind beneath My Wings." I played the piano at that time. Heather bought me the song's sheet music and wrote the sweetest message saying how the song described the way she felt about me.

Heather was most definitely the wind beneath *my* wings.

Heather was beautiful. Heather was just beautiful, not only on the inside, but on the outside too, with dark brown hair, big brown eyes, and beautiful tanned skin. All the boys loved her and would cry on my shoulder when they couldn't figure out why she wouldn't love them back.

Heather loved Jesus. Heather and I loved Jesus, and it didn't matter what denomination we belonged to. Many of our conversations were Christ-centered, and we knew that, with Him in our lives, everything would be okay.

We often compared our friendship to the biblical Jonathan and David friendship.

> *When David had finished speaking with Saul, Jonathan was bound to David in close friendship and loved him as much as he loved himself.* (1 Samuel 18:1 CBS).

Heather had a servant's Heart. Heather had such a heart to serve. If someone needed help, she was there to help them. She collected money for the Salvation Army. She was a part of canned food drives. Heather taught me the importance of showing up. Earning service hours for the various high school clubs we were involved in was never a problem for us.

Death

Now that you have seen the many attributes of Heather, you may be able to understand the impact her accident had on my life.

My first real experience with grief came when I was twenty-one years old. My sister lost her husband in a freak accident. After his death, my sister's world was shattered. I remember thinking about people going about their normal routines, but for me, what was normal changed. The same thing happened for me with Heather's death.

Our friend Norman Boyd was the one who called to tell me about the accident. I remember the phone call vividly.

"I can tell by your cheery voice that you have not heard the news. Heather Knox was killed in a car accident yesterday," he said.

The Process of Emotions

Panic, denial, overwhelming sorrow, and anger were just a few of the many emotions that ran through me. I was so overwhelmed by emotions that I became numb.

Because I love the Knox family so much, I just wanted to be there for them. My body went into autopilot. I went to Pensacola to love on them. I went to all the services held in Heather's honor. I prepared a meal for them. This part was easy for me because I had tasks to focus on. But when all the formalities were complete, the true grieving began, and I was left alone with my emotions.

Anger. I was so mad that this had happened to Heather. Heather was a good person. Doesn't God know about all the horrible people in the world? As callous as it sounds, why didn't God take one of them?

Heather was such an amazing mother. She loved Jakob more than life itself. For over twenty years, I have worked as a school nurse in the public school system, and I have seen horrible parents. Parents who chose their addiction over their children. Parents who neglected their kids, sending them to school hungry and cold.

If the accident hadn't happened, Jakob would have been raised by a loving mother who would have provided him with all the essentials he needed. This wasn't the way life was supposed to go. Heather should still be here, and life should be going on as usual. Mr. and Mrs. Knox should be enjoying grandparenthood, watching Donnie and Heather navigate parenthood together. These were supposed to be happy times.

Anxiety. Heather's accident reminded me how fragile life is. Being a mother was so important to us both. When my children were young, I sometimes worried about what would happen to them if something were to happen to me. I felt like no one would love my children as much as I did, and I wanted to be the one to raise them. Now, look what happened to Heather when Jakob was only nine months old.

Depression. When I'm left alone with my emotions, depression tends to come to the forefront. Depression can make mundane tasks seem difficult. Energy levels fall to zero. The thought of taking a shower seems like preparing to run a marathon. I'll never see Heather again in this earthly lifetime.

I read about how acceptance is the ultimate goal in grieving, but it doesn't mean you have finished grieving. You just accept, finally, that death happened, and there is absolutely nothing you can do about it. I believe grieving is lifelong. Various triggers will make you feel sad, angry, anxious, and so on. This is where you are figuring out your new normal in life.

I'm certain that those of us in the grip of grief share similar thoughts and feelings, yet each of our experiences is deeply personal. Are there lessons to be learned? I think so.

I remember one conversation Heather and I had like it was yesterday. We were seventeen years old, at the beach, and walking along the shoreline. We concluded that we had made it. We had matured as much as we were going to mature. We were ready to take the world by the horns.

Oh, to be seventeen years old again!

We were clueless.

When I was young, I pictured life unfolding like the old television show, *Leave It to Beaver*. I would live in the picture-perfect white house with a white picket fence, money would always be in the bank, and I would always be well and positive.

Spoiler alert: it wasn't.

Life is hard. After Heather died, and many other unexpected hard times, I realized I wasn't handling life well. I needed professional help. Seeing a counselor was one of the best decisions I have ever made. At the time, I struggled to decide because I believed it meant I was weak. I felt like everything I needed to know was in the Bible. I faced opposition from family members too. There was a stigma attached to mental health issues then, but thankfully, that has improved since the 1990s.

In counseling, I learned the difference between ideal and real. As a perfectionist, my goals were always ideal. I came to understand that life will bring some great times, but there will also be bad times. Realistically, your plans and goals will need to be adjusted, regardless of how hard you try to make them work out as initially planned.

Heather's life and death have impacted me in so many ways. Her life taught me to live life big. She taught me the importance of compassion and how to show up for people when they need me. She taught me to surround myself with a tribe of people who truly care for me and make me feel loved and secure. She taught me to take chances and to laugh at myself when I make a mistake.

Her death taught me how fragile life is. I do not take life for granted, and I strive to ensure that all the people I love know how much I care for them. The world will keep spinning after we die, and that is what I want it to do. Now, I couldn't imagine the sun NOT rising.

My faith in God isn't as strong as it was when Heather and I were teenagers, but I still believe in Jesus. We live in an imperfect world with imperfect people. Some relationships are not as I had imagined they would be at this stage of my life, but I have learned that it's okay. I can let go and let God do his work on us all.

In conclusion, what I have learned the most from my time with Heather on earth and from her death in her awful car accident is the poem, "The Dash." This poem, written by Linda Ellis, points out how we "dash" between birth and death. It's often read at funerals. It's a tribute to the one who died, but it also reminds us to make the most of our own dash—to live fully and with purpose.

"The Dash" portrays the way I truly want to live now.

What This Father Learned Through Grief

Even though I've come to realize that my journey through grief will never be complete, I've learned many difficult lessons along the way. I share them here in case they may be helpful to you.

1. Avoid going on the journey of grief alone.

   For me, it proved therapeutic to have Joyce share my thoughts with as a shoulder to cry on. Initially, I attempted to isolate my feelings. All that did was allow my sorrow to build and build into anger for which there was no apparent outlet. It was as though my soul was like a balloon being filled with water until it burst. I discovered that holding open and honest conversations about my feelings helped lessen the emotional pain.

2. Treat living with grief as an ongoing event that requires endurance.

   Running a marathon is a test of physical endurance and takes adequate preparation. Living with grief requires a different form of endurance and a different form of preparation. A marathon is an anticipated event, and, with proper preparation, the run is finished with a feeling of success. Grief, on the other hand, strikes without warning. It leaves its victims feeling helpless, with a lingering need to endure the pain long after the event has passed. I believe that there are not many people who would want to prepare for something as painful as grief. If we tried to anticipate and prepare for a tragedy that may never happen, we would be robbed of joyful living.

When we trust in God and have faith in his ability to sustain us through the worst of circumstances, I believe grief preparation often happens almost by accident.

3. Adapt as if experiencing an amputation.

When a limb is lost or one of our senses is impaired—such as sight or hearing—we learn to adapt and function despite the loss. In a similar but more profound way, the loss of a significant relationship leaves us feeling bewildered and uncertain about what to do. How do I compensate for the gap created by my lost reality?

What is my new reality? Developing one is entirely up to each individual, and the beauty is that, with self-determination, we can cultivate a new perspective tailored to our circumstances. In other words, we can figure out the best course of action to continue living with purpose.

4. Search for opportunities to experience joy.

All manners of memories fill our lives. Memory details may fade, but I believe the emotion accompanying a memory remains with us. It's important to expect that memories will surprise us at unusual times. Words, pictures, art, and observations may spark them. Basically, anything our five senses can detect can evoke a memory. A great memory can lift us out of despair and transport us to a happier time. Memories become our treasures.

5. Find Sources of energy.

   Grief can sap us of physical and emotional energy, and, as a result, we may succumb to self-pity. If we want to live full lives, it's essential to prevent this from happening. Take, for example, a car that is poorly maintained. If we neglect our vehicle, it will spend a lot of time in the garage. It's much the same for us, except that the components needing maintenance include our bodies, minds, and spirits. Exactly how to approach maintenance is a matter of personal choice, but it's crucial to our continued well-being.

6. Overcome the temptation to quit.

   Living with grief creates a significant life change. Successfully dealing with this change or any major change is not easy and takes dedication. The ability to develop a long-lasting relationship with someone close to us requires discipline, patience, consistency, and understanding. To make a relationship work, we must be willing to put in the effort and do whatever it takes. Living with grief is like that. But now, we must build a new relationship with something very real yet intangible. So, the principles applied to building a long-lasting personal relationship are still applicable. At the very least, we know we did our best and will continue to thrive despite our inability to feel any measure of success.

Epilogue

Our family story continues to unfold. Sharing it would not have been possible without the efforts of those who allowed me to coerce them into playing a part. There were no bribes, and they all did their part voluntarily, albeit reluctantly. Undoubtedly, we will share this journey with future generations.

It's my sincere hope that these reflections will serve as a guiding beacon for others who are struggling in the grip of grief. The collateral emotional damage of Heather's death is on display, but thankfully, our family's grief experience has not prevented us from learning, moving forward, and living with joy.

Individually, our experiences have instilled sensitivity and compassion for others who are hurting. Over time, we came to realize that grief will always be our unwanted companion, but we do not let this companion color our continued journey with dread. Instead, we learn to let our grief mold us into better people by embracing it.

What does our family tragedy teach us? All I can say is that, for me, the wound remains after twenty-five-plus years. Scars will always be present, but they don't have to be debilitating. When the family and friends who have partnered with me on this journey surround me, we happily reminisce about our experiences and recall the great times we've had together.

Some friendships dissolved, primarily because some people weren't sure what to say around us. Their lives continued, and they faced their own challenges. Although life seems surreal as we grieve, life as usual continues for those around us. We may feel like observers watching a drama unfold from a distance, bystanders who are not part of the play.

Soon after grief entered my life, I desperately wanted to find an escape from the pain. One night, I sat alone at the beach and sobbed. I noticed the surf gently rolling under a clear sky with an abundant array of stars. A group of adolescents giggled as they shone their flashlights over the shore searching for marine life that only appears at night. I was amazed that people could be happy, and that life could continue around me.

In that moment, I realized how selfish it would be of me to want other people to experience my pain. Those of us impacted by grief—like anyone else—have the ability of self-determination. We have the choice of succumbing to destructive stimuli or deriving lessons to help us live full and productive lives.

I think it's safe to say that, despite grief's scars, we choose not to be shackled with anything that will hold us back.

Heather's Legacy

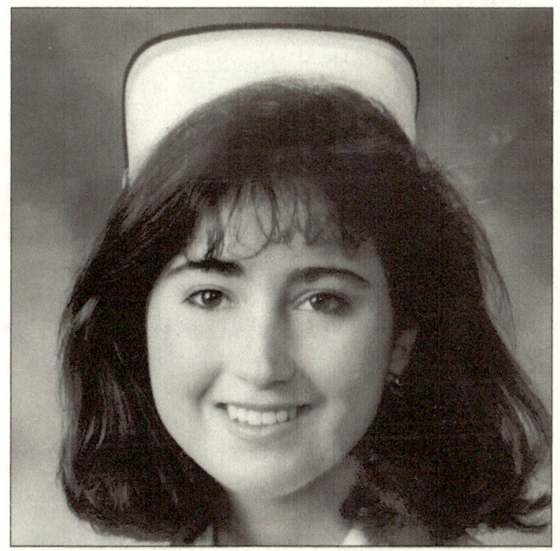

Nurse Heather, the epitome of a care giver.

Sacred Heart Hospital in Pensacola, where Heather worked as a pediatric nurse, named a home healthcare program for children, "Just for Kids," in Heather's honor.

In 2008, Heather's cousin Debbie and her former husband established a $100,000 endowed scholarship for rising juniors participating full-time in Lipscomb University's nursing program. Students with loans of more than half the cost of attending the university receive preference for the award, which they present every other year.

The Heather Knox Barber Nursing Scholarship also encourages recipients to participate in medical missions. Doing so echoes Heather's Christian concern for others and her participation in medical missions in Nigeria and Guyana. Each semester, Chelsia Harris, Executive Director of the School of Nursing at David Lipscomb University in Nashville, Tennessee, announces the recipient of the Heather Knox Barber Award with the following introduction:

> Heather Knox Barber, the daughter of Joyce and Tom Knox, was a nurse, and not just any nurse. Heather was a joyful nurse who dedicated her life to the compassionate care of her patients in the United States and abroad. Heather was patient, gentle, kind, and peaceful. She served her patients and their families with integrity, humility, and patience. Unfortunately, Heather lost her life in a fatal car accident on May 27, 1999. Since that time, Heather's family has made it their mission to inspire and encourage the next generation of nurses to embrace their calling with joy and peace, to serve with compassion, to lead with humility, and to love without conditions. In memory and honor of Heather Knox Barber, her family has chosen to honor one nursing student each semester, who, in the eyes of their faculty, staff, and administration, has demonstrated these qualities and characteristics throughout nursing school.

Resources

Songs

"Precious Child" by Karen Taylor Good

"God Will Take Care of You" by Rosemary Siemens

"Trust and Obey" by Don Moen

"Go Rest High on That Mountain" by Vince Gill

"Wind Beneath My Wings" by Bette Midler

"Going Home," Largo movement of Antonín Dvořák's Symphony No. 9 in E Minor ("From the New World"), sung by Sissel Kyrkjebø

"The Last Goodbye" by Billy Boyd.

"Father and Son" by Cat Stephens

"Fathers and Daughters" by Michael Bolton

"Mothers and Daughters" by Emma White

Reading Material

The Grieving Christian by Zig Ziglar.

Streams in the Desert by Mrs. Charles Cowen.

"Step by Step," a poem by Barbara Cornet Ryberg.

"The Dash," a poem by Linda Ellis.

"Remember Me," a poem by Margaret Mead

Small Group

Compassionate Friends www.compasssionatefriends.org

Scriptures

All Scriptures are NIV, Unless Otherwise Noted

Ecclesiastes 4:9-12

Exodus 17:8-13

Matthew 6:25-34

Deuteronomy 6:4-9

Luke 15

Psalm 139

Jeremiah 18:1-6

Romans 12:1-2

1 Samuel 18:1

Something to Enjoy

Heather's Recipe for Cypress Inn Muffins

These muffins are a family favorite, and the recipe has been shared countless times with family and friends.

How Heather was able to convince the owner of the Cypress Inn (closed indefinitely) in Tuscaloosa, Alabama, to share the recipe is beyond me. ENJOY!

1 – 15oz box of Raisin Bran1 – tsp cloves
3 – cups sugar1- tsp nutmeg
5 – cups all-purpose flower
4 – eggs
2 – tsp salt
1 – cup oil
5 – tsp soda
1 – qt buttermilk
2 – tsp cinnamon
2 – tsp vanilla

Preheat oven to 400°F. Mix all dry ingredients in a large bowl. Add remaining ingredients and mix well.

Place in a greased muffin tin. Bake 10 – 15 mins. The batter will last for up to four weeks in the refrigerator.

Acknowledgments

This book has been on my heart for a very long time. Despite my best efforts to stay focused, I struggled to maintain a consistent writing pace. The embers continually burned, but there was no flame until I met Beth McLaughlin.

I would be remiss if I failed to thank Beth for guiding me in writing this story. She has more patience than most people I know, and, through her persistence, this book has become a reality. I knew that I would need someone with the proper skill set to help me complete this task. Coincidentally, I met Beth at St. Christopher's Episcopal Church in Pensacola, Florida, in the spring of 2022. As I got to know her on a deeper level, I realized she was the perfect person to ask, because I knew she would be honest. Consequently, I asked her in the fall of 2023 to be my editorial sidekick. She accepted before she knew what she was getting into.

During the twenty-five years of compiling our family story, we have been surrounded by countless people who have played a role in helping to lessen the grip grief has on us. Specifically, I want to thank Joyce, Scott, Donnie, Jamie, Debbie, Mary Ann, and Angela, whose narratives were invaluable to me as this labor of love came to fruition. Without their love and support, completing this family memoir would have been impossible.

www.ingramcontent.com/pod-product-compliance
Lightning Source LLC
LaVergne TN
LVHW091011080826
845145LV00003B/1219

* 9 7 8 1 9 6 9 9 3 5 2 8 2 *